R.19-95

EGYPTI

An examination of the r
of magical practices in
Egypt by a member of tl
Golden Dawn.

In this series
THE BOOK OF SPLENDOURS
  Eliphas Lévi
THE CHALDEAN ORACLES OF ZOROASTER
  Introduction by Kathleen Raine
THE DREAM OF SCIPIO (SOMNIUM SCIPIONIS)
  Introduction by Robert Temple
THE GREAT SECRET
  Eliphas Lévi
THE HEPTARCHIA MYSTICA OF JOHN DEE
  Edited by Robert Turner
THE MYSTERIES OF THE QABALAH
  Eliphas Lévi
THE QABALAH
  Papus

EGYPTIAN MAGIC

by

Florence Farr

Introduction by Timothy d'Arch Smith

THE AQUARIAN PRESS
Wellingborough, Northamptonshire

First published in the 'Collectanea
Hermetica' series 1896
This Edition first published 1982
Third Impression 1985

© THE AQUARIAN PRESS 1982
Introduction © TIMOTHY D'ARCH SMITH 1982

This book is sold subject to the condition that it shall not, by way of trade or otherwise, be lent, re-sold, hired out, or otherwise circulated without the publisher's prior consent in any form of binding or cover other than that in which it is published and without a similar condition including this condition being imposed on the subsequent purchaser.

British Library Cataloguing in Publication Data

Farr, Florence
  Egyptian magic: occult mysteries in Ancient
  Egypt.
  1. Magic, Egyptian
  I. Title
  133.4'0932   BF1591

ISBN 0-85030-277-3

Printed and bound in Great Britain.

PREFACE TO THE 'COLLECTANEA HERMETICA' SERIES

In 1875 the creation of the Theosophical Society offered a way of escape for those seekers after Truth who could accept neither a dogmatic brand of Christianity nor a dull and barren Rationalism, and for whom Spiritualism was intellectually inadequate. For a decade Madame Blavatsky's emphasis on Eastern religion and thought was enough, but a growing number of English members sought to study—in both theory and practice—the Hermetic Tradition of the West. Their demands were finally met in 1887 by the founding of the Hermetic Order of the Golden Dawn, a secret Order based upon the precepts and practices of the Rosicrucians of the seventeenth century, and whose members were required to follow a disciplined course of study. With a high proportion of articulate and cultured men and women among its members it was inevitable that the Golden Dawn should produce lasting memorials, and while the splendid rituals created by S.L.M. Mathers are the best known of these, the true value of the Order appeared in the series of manuals edited by the Order's founder, William Wynn Westcott.

The ten volumes of Westcott's *Collectanea Hermetica* appeared over the three years from 1893 to 1896 when the Golden Dawn was at its peak. It was a remarkable series providing guides for the public and, virtually, textbooks for members on almost all the major pursuits of the Order: on Alchemy, the Qabalah, Gnosticism, the Mystery Religions and Egyptian traditions. In every volume the intellectual integrity of the authors is evident, as is an eagerness to bring academic respectability to subjects derided by their contemporaries. Westcott and his colleagues were pioneers in the study of 'rejected knowledge', and the gradual acceptance today of the real value of research in such fields is a vindication of their efforts and justification enough for the long overdue rescue of their work from an ill-deserved neglect.

R. A. GILBERT

THE PARTS OF A HUMAN BEING.

THE PARTS OF A HUMAN BEING.

Determinative.	Egyptian Name.	Equivalent in English.
A Fish	Khat or Kat	Body, Corpse.
A Mummy and a Seal	Sahu	Elemental Body, Astral Body.
An Upright Snake	Tet or Zet	Spiritual Body, Soul.
A Fan	Khaibt	Radiations of the Sahu; the Sphere or Aura, Emanation, Odour, etc.
The Forepart of a Lion	Hati	Executant, Human heredity, Habit, Instinct.
A Vessel with Ears as Handles	Aub or Ab	The Will, similar to the animal Will, but containing within it the germs of the Spirit and Human Ego, in the form of an Egg and a concave receptacle.
The Upraised Hands	Kai or Ka	The Individuality, the Human Ego.
A Hawk, Heron or Ram	Ba or Baie	The penetrating Mind, the link with the Divine.
The Bennu Bird	KhouKhu, or Yckh	The Magical powers. The Shining one. The Augoeides of Greek philosophy.
The Radiating Sun	Hammemit	The Unborn Soul; apparently a separate emanation of the Solar Light.

INTRODUCTION

Florence Farr (1860-1917) was the youngest, very much the youngest, of the five children of William Farr, a colleague of Florence Nightingale (in whose memory he presumably named his youngest child), a man who combined a talent for medicine with a genius for statistics. The death of Florence's mother when she was sixteen and of her father seven years later gave her an early if involuntary foretaste of the emancipation that satisfied her so much in adulthood. She continued her education, regularly at first, then less so, finally giving it up altogether. For a short while she became a teacher under the delusion, still common today, that those whose formal studies have been abandoned or performed without noticeable merit are better prepared to instruct the young than qualified scholars. Her aspirations then turned to the stage, an arena where her talent and her beauty procured her fame and love and led her in to the occult society that was the inspiration for the book reprinted here.

Florence was a woman of many parts, eager to learn and to distribute the fruits of her learning. W. B. Yeats compared her mind with the game of spillikins, a bundle of different coloured sticks all muddled together. With Florence you never knew which coloured stick of knowledge she might suddenly withdraw from her sheaf. Ezra Pound, who met Florence in America with the philanthropist John Quinn, observed the same thing:

> One comes to you
> And takes strange gain away:
> Trophies fished up; some curious suggestion;
> Fact that leads nowhere; and a tale or two
> Pregnant with mandrakes . . .

She was musical, musical enough to tour America with Arnold Dolmetsch where she spoke verse to Dolmetsch's accompaniment on a specially-designed psaltery—an evening's entertainment that one cannot help feeling did not always play to packed houses—although Dolmetsch had considerable reservations about her talent. She learned embroidery from William Morris's daughter, May. She wrote a novel, some plays reflecting her fascination with ancient Egypt, and a book on female emancipation, her brief marriage to Edward Emery, one of the famous family of actors, having convinced her of the boredom of household drudgeries and the tiresomeness, not to say actual detestation of, physical love when unaccompanied by mutual admiration.

She had a certain administrative capacity, evidenced by her managership of the Avenue Theatre, her position as Scribe in the Order of the Golden Dawn and her eventual assumption of the Principalship of a girls' school in Ceylon, but her incorrigibly 'flighty' attitude to affairs of the heart spilled over in to her everyday life. Her talent on the stage never rose to genius; her musical ability remained secondrate and there were grave faults in her managerial duties at Golden Dawn headquarters. Her letters from Ceylon, too, exhibit her inherent laziness and she speaks, not of the workaday problems of superintending a boarding school in a foreign land, but of her idyllic existence, the availability of a victoria and a motor car to run her about the island and of the exotic odour she exuded owing to her consumption twice a day of spicy curries.

There remained, always, her charm and her beauty, 'her large eyes and crescent eyebrows and a smile', and her 'spillikins' of knowledge on which she could draw to entertain and attract her audience. If someone wanted to talk spooks, she would talk them; if they turned the conversation to music or the theatre, she was ready for them. Furthermore, if a man wanted to make love to her, that, too, came very easily. By 1894 she had, according to George Bernard Shaw, a list of fourteen lovers.

Shaw and Yeats came in to her life at much the same time, in 1890, at Bedford Park, a red-brick London suburb teeming with cockroaches and Bohemians not far from where she had lived with her unsatisfactory husband from whom, now, she had been separated for two years without troubling to instigate divorce proceedings. Coincidentally, several Golden Dawn members lived there and coincidentally again, although occultists would not say so, there is still a Golden Dawn tradition in Bedford Park. The Yeats family had come to London from Ireland (for the second time) in 1887 and had moved to Bedford Park, perhaps to be near the Morris family who lived in

XI

Hammersmith, the following year. Yeats saw Florence in a play, *A Sicilian Idyll,* written by an Irish doctor, John Todhunter, who 'looked exactly like God in an illustrated family Bible', and much admired her rendering of the verse. They were drawn together by a mutual interest in the occult. Florence, like Yeats, had been studying such matters for some time, certainly for ten years, since she noted, on quitting her education, that her horoscope was auspicious for such a decision. Yeats had begun with Theosophy, a cult that was sweeping England, appealing not only to the genuine seeker but also to the fashionably giddy and empty-headed as Spiritualism had done some years before; but he was interested in the physical phenomena of mysticism and these, as Madame Blavatsky herself had stated, were not to be found in the Theosophical Society. However, the Society's journal, *Lucifer,* included a veiled reference to another society where such things were being investigated—the Hermetic Order of the Golden Dawn.

Yeats was initiated into the Golden Dawn in March 1890 and introduced Florence later the same year. For both of them advancement in the Order came swiftly. It was the Order, more than anything else, that was the link between them. Whether they were in love with each other is unclear. Yeats's sisters suspected so and Yeats himself records that Florence was the only person in his life to whom he could tell everything. This need not be taken as evidence of any greater intimacy. Probably they had a brief affair, but Florence's insincerity about matters of the heart—at any protestation of affection she was inclined to become 'stagy' and affected—and her rejection of the institution of marriage would, for Yeats, have made it a transitory association. In any case, another woman, Maud Gonne, came into Yeats's life and Florence found herself involved with a man in every way different from Yeats and one who demonstrably did fall in love with her: George Bernard Shaw.

Shaw was among the first-night audience of *A Sicilian Idyll* and was as impressed as Yeats by Florence's talent. He was involved with several other women at the time but was soon seeing Florence every day. He had a fascination for married women and liked to insinuate himself in to married households, not really to carry off the bride but to woo her at a distance. He had, too, long been obsessed with the 'emancipated' woman and with a desire to prove to the public that actresses were not habitually loose women but honest, hardworking, people getting on with their careers. To find an emancipated woman who was also an actress and, at his instigation, a divorcee, was the

XII

fulfilment of several dreams at once. Not that Shaw was a dreamer (as Yeats was): he was a fighter, diligent and high minded and, regardless of his passion for Florence, he began a ruthless grooming of her as an actress, particularly as an interpreter of the female roles in the plays of Ibsen.

To be fair to Florence, there were good reasons why she accepted, indeed actively encouraged, the attentions of Yeats and Shaw; and, to be fair to them, equally good reasons for their finding her unsatisfactory. She shared with Yeats a fascination for magic, with Shaw a love of the theatre and an ambition, at least the semblance of an ambition, to become a great actress. Yeats, however, disliked her facile mind and her ingrained artificiality, which were probably the attributes, if only they could have been tamed to his liking, that appealed to Shaw. Shaw, in his turn, despised occult pursuits, was appalled by their irrationality. Florence would not, more likely could not, keep silent to Shaw about them. At her home he would have seen her paintings of Egyptian gods and goddesses, although not, it is to be hoped, her magical weapons and temple regalia, and he knew of *Egyptian Magic:* 'You would not believe in my doctrine of working at some reality every day' he railed at her; 'but you none the less worked every day at your unreality. And now you think to undo the work of all those years by a phrase and a shilling's worth of exoteric Egyptology.' Nevertheless it is hard to believe that Shaw was not thinking a little of Florence when he wrote *Caesar and Cleopatra.*

Shaw and Yeats continued to write parts for her in their plays, Shaw some very fine ones, but a rift was inevitable. Florence felt more for the Golden Dawn than she did for the exhausting hobby-horses Shaw kept badgering her to ride. Shaw knew this perfectly well, sheered off, retrenched elsewhere, blotted her from his mind. In old age he could not even remember having written to her, although several letters survive. Yeats bowed out too, but intellectually the Golden Dawn kept them together. It was the Order that let them down finally, not the other way round. They were both victims of an internecine war they were powerless to oppose.

Florence's *Egyptian Magic,* issued in 1896 over her Golden Dawn motto initials, S.S.D.D. ('Sapientia Sapienti Dona Data': 'Wisdom is given as a gift to the wise') was number 8 of a nine-volume sequence of occult tracts, 'Collectanea Hermetica'. Edited by William Wynn Westcott, head of the Golden Dawn, the series, while not required reading for Order members, is unquestionably doctrinaire. All the Golden Dawn rituals are redolent with Egyptian symbolism and it is with this in mind, together with Florence's insistence on the efficacy of practical magic, that the book must be read. Slight though it may appear today, even a little pretentious in its lengthy translations from Gnostic fragments of which there were after all French versions already in print but included perhaps because of the similarity of some of the 'barbarous names of evocation' to the Enochian language taught to Golden Dawn members, it is nevertheless a pioneering book. The science of Egyptology was only just coming of age. The OED does not record a use of the word before 1859. Although there was, at the time Florence produced her book, a Professorship at London University, it had been established solely for the magisterial Flinders Petrie. There would be no academic foundation at Oxford for another five years and Cambridge would have to wait over a quarter of a century longer. Yet, strangely, it was from Cambridge that the three greatest English Egyptologists came: Charles Wycliffe Goodwin, E.A. Wallis Budge and Herbert Thompson. Of these, the studies of Wallis Budge were the most important for Florence and for the Golden Dawn, for in 1892 Budge had been appointed Acting Keeper of the Egyptian department in the British Museum, around the corner from the Golden Dawn's London temple, and had been elevated to Principal Keeper in 1894. It is rumoured that he was not unsympathetic to Order pursuits and probably aided members in their researches. Florence would have been proud that her book on Egyptian Magic preceded that of Budge's by two years.

This is not the place to iterate the story of the establishment of the Golden Dawn, its schisms and its eventual demise. That can be found in several other places. Suffice it to say that its foundations, laid on the twin quicksands of a forged charter and an arrogant sacerdotalism, were bound to subside, yet not before there had been recruited in to it some splendid and genuine minds: Florence herself, Yeats, Allan Bennett (with whom Florence summoned to visible appearance the spirit of Mercury), the Order's bugbear, Aleister Crowley (who much admired Florence) and its uncanny tutelary genius, Samuel Liddell MacGregor Mathers. In 1897, the Order's founder and the forger of its charter, W. W. Westcott, was rumbled as being a practising magician. As well as having a financial interest in the Sanitary Wood Wool Company —

perhaps some precursor to Chilprufe—he was also a Coroner. There was no hint of necromantic practices in the Golden Dawn, but to the unversed minds of Westcott's superiors such a suspicion occurred. As Aleister Crowley pointed out, he was employed to sit on corpses not to raise them and he found it prudent to resign. This left Mathers as Head of the Order, quite rightly so, since he and his clairvoyant wife, the sister of the French philosopher Henri Bergson, had written most of the rituals; but their ill-timed decision to go to live in Paris, from where his autocracy in all Order matters became almost megalomaniacal, left remaining London members with a quantity of pricks against which to kick. Mathers refused to yield his authority to anyone else and expelled several recalcitrant members, Florence, originally his London representative, among them. The London Temple members defiantly reconstituted the Order without him and Florence became its Scribe, responsible for various administrative tasks and for examining candidates, but she soon found herself in as much trouble with the new regime as she had been with Mathers. Miss Annie Horniman, who had supported Mathers financially and had put up the money for Florence to produce the season of plays at the Avenue Theatre which had included Yeats's *Land of Heart's Desire* and Shaw's *Arms and the Man*, disapproved of the somewhat slapdash methods Florence was employing in her duties. Squabbles continued to break out intermittently and eventually Florence resigned.

With hindsight, what is interesting is that the Order does seem to have been established *sub specie aeternitatis*. Its rituals are still performed, its philosophies still much admired. If, as Yeats alleged, there is any truth in 'the practice and philosophy of what we have agreed to call magic, in what I must call the evocation of spirits', the Golden Dawn system is still the most efficacious; but there must be harmony and a singleness of purpose. To quote Yeats again: 'If we preserve the unity of the Order, if we make that unity efficient among us, the Order will become a single very powerful talisman.' This was not to be. The system demanded a formal, disciplined training with overseers to be respected and laws to be obeyed. It was not founded to be run on the 'progressive' lines of its reconstitution where every member did much as he liked, formed groups within it (as Florence founded one, for the purposes of skrying in the Tree of Life), bent the rules and altered the curriculum. The dangers of such an approach to any educational system are obvious.

If Mathers had stayed put and had displayed the smallest tinge of humility who knows to what heights the Order might have risen; but Florence, at loggerheads with both her original Chief and the new administration had had enough. Her departure for Ceylon in 1912 can be seen as a symbolic shaking off of the Order's dust from her feet. Her co-magician, Allan Bennett, had made the same journey, for the same reasons, perhaps had even paved the way for her new appointment. Many of her friends begged her not to go, but she would not listen. Yeats particularly mourned her departure and wrote sadly in *A Vision* that she

> Preferred to teach a school
> Away from neighbour and friend
> Among dark skins, and there
> Permit foul years to wear
> Hidden from eyesight, to the unnoticed end.

TIMOTHY D'ARCH SMITH

BOOKS BY, OR WITH CONTRIBUTIONS BY, FLORENCE FARR

A Short Enquiry concerning the Hermetic Art. By a Lover of Philalethes . . . An introduction to alchemy and notes by S.S.D.D. (Theosophical Society, 1894). 'Collectanea Hermetica', Vol. 3.

The Dancing Faun (Mathews & Lane, 1894).

The Beloved of Hathor and The Shrine of the Golden Hawk. By Florence Farr and Olivia Shakespear [Croydon, E. G. Craig, c.1895].

PHILALETHES EUGENIUS [pseud., i.e. Thomas Vaughan], *Euphrates . . . with a Commentary by S.S.D.D.* (Theosophical Society, 1896). 'Collectanea Hermetica', Vol. 7.

The Way of Wisdom. An Investigation of the Meanings of the Hebrew Alphabet considered as a Remnant of Chaldean Wisdom (J. M. Watkins, 1900).

The Mystery of Time: a Masque (Theosophical Society, 1905).

The Music of Speech, containing the Words of some Poets, Thinkers and Musicmakers regarding the Practice of the Bardic Art, together with Fragments of Verse set to its own Melody by Florence Farr (E. Mathews, 1909).

A Calendar of Philosophy. Edited by Florence Farr from the Works of the Great Writers (Palmer, 1910).

Modern Woman: her Intentions (Palmer, 1910).

The Solemnization of Jacklin: some Adventures on the Search for Reality (Fifield, 1912).

SELECTED FURTHER READING

BAX (Clifford, editor), *Florence Farr, Bernard Shaw, W. B. Yeats: Letters* (Home & van Thal, 1947).

FINNERAN (Richard J. and others, editors), *Letters to W. B. Yeats*, 2 vols (Macmillan, 1977).

GLANVILLE (S. R. K.), *The Growth and Nature of Egyptology* (Cambridge University Press, 1947).

HARPER (George Mills), *Yeats's Golden Dawn* (Macmillan, 1974).

HOWE (Ellic), *The Magicians of the Golden Dawn: a Documentary History of a Magical Order 1887-1923* (Routledge & Kegan Paul, 1972).

JOHNSON (Josephine), *Florence Farr: Bernard Shaw's 'New Woman'* (Colin Smythe, 1975).

KING (Francis), *Ritual Magic in England 1887 to the Present Day* (Spearman, 1970).

XVII

PETERS (Margot), *Bernard Shaw and the Actresses* (New York, Doubleday, 1980).

TUOHY (Frank), *Yeats* (Macmillan, 1976).

EGYPTIAN MAGIC.

By S. S. D. D.

The study of Magic, which has now fallen into disrepute was, among the Egyptians, regarded with a veneration hardly accorded to the highest Philosophy in modern times.

To the Ancient Egyptians the most eminent man was he who had by hard training gained supremacy over the Elements, from which his own body and the Manifested World were alike formed; one whose Will had risen Phœnix-like from the ashes of his desires; one whose Intuition, cleansed from the stains of material illusion, was a clear mirror in which he could perceive the Past, the Present and the Future.

The Kings and Priests of Egypt were the elect of those who had studied with success in the " School of Wisdom," a Philosophical Aristocracy; they were chosen because they were not only wise, but could use their wisdom. They could give strength to the armies of the nation and they had the means of transmitting their power; for the Staff of the " King-Initiate " held so strong a magical potency, that, with it in his hand, the leader of armies became as mighty as Pharaoh himself.

The King-Priests gave forth an exoteric religion to the people, by which to guide their footsteps until they had reached that stage of development (it may have been only after repeated failures, incarnation after incarnation), when they also might join the ranks of the initiated: yet it appears extremely probable that the whole Egyptian population was allowed a certain participation in the Mysteries; for the tests of a candidate before Initiation were of such a nature that none but human beings developed to a considerable degree of perfection could hope to stand them.

There is every reason to suppose that only those who had received some grade of initiation were mummified; for it is certain that, in the eyes of the Egyptians, mummification effectually prevented reincarnation. Reincarnation was necessary to imperfect souls, to those who had failed to pass the tests of initiation; but for those who had the Will and the capacity to enter the Secret Adytum, there was seldom necessity for that liberation of the soul which is said to be effected by the destruction of the body.

The body of the Initiate was therefore preserved after death as a species of Talisman or material basis for the manifestation of the Soul upon earth.

In studying Egyptian Magic one has at once a thoroughly scientific satisfaction. One is troubled with no vague theories, but receives precise practical details; we observe that every square inch of the Upper and Under Worlds is mapped out. The strength that such a system inherently contains was proved by the long duration of the archaic Egyptian civilization.

The first principles of Egyptian Magic were based on an elaborate system of correspondences depending on the formula that, the evolution of what is material follows the type and symbol of the emanation of the spiritual; that spirit and matter are opposite faces of the self-same mystery.* The Egyptian Adepts regarded the conceptions of the mind, the aspirations of the soul, the words of the mouth and the functions of the body, as

* See Westcott on Kabalah, in *Lucifer*, May, 1893, p. 204, and Tyndall, Belfast Address.

possessing analogies from which a complete system of rules of life and death could be constructed. Moreover they looked upon each body, or manifested being, as the material basis of a long vista of immaterial entities functioning as Spirit, Soul and Mind in the Formative, Creative and Archetypal Worlds.

Included in this volume is a list of standard works upon the subject of "Egyptian Beliefs," for the use of those who have not studied the modern theories on the subject; so there is no need to enter here into details which can easily be found elsewhere. I shall therefore at once state the ideas which my study of ancient lore has led me to formulate, without waiting to quote the hypotheses set forth by our leading Egyptologists.

In the first place we have hitherto written of man as composed of soul and body; but the Initiated Egyptians regarded themselves as being far from simply soul and body. They gave names to several human faculties, and postulated for each a possibility of separate existence.

The KHAT, KAT, or Body, was only a vehicle or material basis for the operations of the Ego upon this plane of human earth-life.

In considering the Egyptian philosophy of the Life Cycle, let us start from the beginning; according to the obelisk of Queen Hatshepsu, a human HAMMEMIT or Primal Entity circled round the sun for a period of One Hundred and Twenty Years before incarnation. During this period certain cosmic and elemental forces would be more powerful than others; these environing the Primal Entity would give it a certain characteristic bias, and guide it in the choice of the means and moment of incarnation. In the meantime the reflections of the higher elemental forces affecting the Primal Entity would be at work in the material world. These reflections would bias the human parents in like manner. When the natal epoch arrived the Great Mother-Force, symbolized by the vulture holding the Seal, imprinted upon the Primal

Entity the symbols dominant at the selected moment; and this is the rationale of the Astrological horoscope.

The human mother had in the meantime become the centre of elemental forces that formulated an illusive attraction around her. This is the formulation of the SAHU, or the Astral body of the future human being, under the magic of the natural elemental forces. For the plainest woman, for a time, becomes beautiful in the eyes of her lover. No sooner, however, is the co-operation of the parent forces accomplished than the SAHU hastily attaches itself to the vitalized germ and remains with it as an invisible pattern towards which solid matter gravitating forms the material body. This operation of the Sahu accounts for the vision which some clairvoyants have perceived in regard to the Vegetable Kingdom, of an astral plant-form attached to seeds or grains before they are sown in the ground.

The elemental body then having concentrated round the vitalized ovum, leaves the human mother in her natural state, stripped of the illusive beauty it had imparted to her: and she does not, or should not, regain her specially attractive power until she has done her part by the human being she is about to foster.

We see then that the unborn child is prepared for its emergence into life by the parents who contribute the principle called by the Egyptians the HATI or "whole heart." That is, the Seat of the Inherited instincts racial and individual; including such functions as digestion, hearing, seeing, smelling, and so on. In one word the HATI is the heredity. It is clothed by a body formulated by elemental forces, the SAHU. The SAHU, or astral body, both before and after conception, possessed that power of radiation which formed the sphere of attraction round the human mother, which was sealed by the great Vulture-Mother-Force at the time of conception, and was withdrawn instantly to form the sphere or aura of the future human being—this is called the KHAIBT, or radiating aura.

At the moment of birth the "Ego" joins the body, and there are extant many pictures (dating from the period of the highest Egyptian civilization) which show the birth of great princes; in these the double forms of the Celestially and Terrestrially generated bodies are recognisable. This is to say the circling HAMMEMIT now throws off an emanation which is called the KA or double of the new-born child, and this forms its link with the earthly body by means of another principle, the AB. The HATI is always spoken of in Egyptian texts as associated with the AB or Heart. Just as we, in our conversation, often confuse and combine our instinct and will. Will is a quality latent in every animal; it can in man be developed and cultivated until it becomes Free Will. In the same way the AB (will) or Red Vessel of the Heart is represented in the *Book of the Dead* as containing an egg, and a concave germ: when this concave germ is developed by cultivation the real life and full development of the Ego could begin: that is to say the KA could progress in its celestial evolution, just as the body could progress in its terrestrial evolution.

Of course in thousands of cases the celestial body was restricted; the fatal moment of conception loaded the terrestrial being (composed of the SAHU, HATI, and AB within the KAB or material body) with chains of destiny too strong for him to break through. And the KA or Ego had to return to the HAMMEMIT in the Place of Spirits and await the time when it might again have a chance of regenerating matter Astral and Material, and become of the number of these "Shining Ones," who are set like Jewels in the Diadem of the LORD OF SPIRIT AND LIFE, MADE ONE.

In this conception we have at once the explanation of the dogma regarding the sacrifice of self to self. For the KA or Ego can only grow and become potent through ardent and patient perseverance and struggle.

"Three days I hung upon the Cross, my Self a Sacrifice unto myself," says the God of the Eddas.

"Ich bin nichts in mir. Ichts in dir, und leben in deinem Ichts aus Nichts, lebe du doch in mir, und bringe mich aus dem Ichts in dir," said the German Mystic.

The Man who cannot "be Himself" must be melted down in the casting-ladle of PHTHA. The artist-craftsman of the Gods will disperse the elemental material which in its present combination cannot, and will not, be regenerated; he bides his time for a happier moment of operation.

We have Christ enunciating this doctrine in the parable of the Talents, St. Luke, xix. 26, "Unto every one which hath shall be given, and from him that hath not, even that he hath shall be taken away from him."

This old Egyptian Doctrine is to be discovered again in Matthew Arnold's sonnet on "Immortality:"

"No, no, the energy of life may be
Kept on beyond the grave, but not begun,
And he who flagged not in the earthly strife
From strength to strength advancing, only he
His soul well knit and all his battles won,
Mounts, and that hardly, to eternal life."

Having dwelt for some period on that dark side of the Egyptian Faith which dooms the impotent soul to extinction; I will proceed to discuss the career opened before those who, taking the reins of the chariot of life in their own hands, guide the elemental forces which are linked to that vehicle, safe to the desirable goal.

The seeds placed within the heart or AB may now be considered as symbolising the powers of Thought and Will: these once set in action by Theurgic practices or self-devotion to the highest aspiration of the conscious being produce a curious result. Remembering that in the representations of the AB the principles are reversed as though reflected in a vessel of blood—the concave germ being uppermost. We can then see that the two ends of the concave mass stretch round and form a receptacle for the egg: this symbolises a more quintessential influx from the primal entity or HAMMEMIT descending upon the upstretched arms of the KA in the form of the Hawk or Baie. The Cultivation of Thought and Will is again shown by the uplifted hands in the hieroglyph which represents the KA: and the attitude of aspiration enables it to formulate a resting-place for the piercing, penetrating spirit, the BAIE. This latter principle is represented in four ways; by a hawk crowned, or the HORUS BAIE; by a human-headed hawk; by a Bennu bird or by a ram. The BAIE (spirit) can operate through the egg-like principle contained in the AB and the KA (human Ego) through the concave principle.

These four hieroglyphs used for the word Baie showed distinct orders or genera of souls; for instance, the hawk-soul is only represented as resting upon the KA of the King or Queen. It is called the Royal Soul. The human-headed hawk hovers over the mummies of great initiates and doubtless represents the soul after the incarnation had ceased; its human head is the symbol of the quintessence of the human individuality which the bird bears to the Abode of Blessed Souls.

The BAIE represented by the ram would be the progressive, penetrating power which breaks down barriers and enables the energised human soul to pass into regions, the guardians of which could hold their own against meeker enquiry.

The Bennu bird also is remarkable for transfixing and piercing its prey. There is considerable difficulty about this hieroglyph; if it represents the phœnix as it has been commonly supposed to do, it would be easy to understand that it was the symbol of a soul belonging to a more complex range of being, only to be evolved through a long series of labours on the part of its human counterpart; but if it is simply a form of a common hernshaw I should take it as implying a milder and less fiery nature in the soul.

The ram head is often placed on the stone scarabæus (symbol of self-creation) which replaces the heart in the body of a mummy; representing what the mediæval mystics meant when they talked of the "Stone of the Wise." That is, the Will which had become self-creative and was united eternally to its celestial, progressive, penetrative faculty. The consecrated Will and purified Thought of the true Magus.

In the first Egyptian Room at the British Museum a painting, said to be of Queen Hatshepset, who lived about B.C. 1600, is hung on the walls (the Queen's name has been painted out and that of Thothmes III. substituted), she is making perfume offerings; this picture is reproduced from an obelisk now fallen, which was set up by this Queen at Karnak. A print of this painting is reproduced in the English translation of Wiedemann's *Immortality of the Soul*.

Here we have a representation of a fully initiated ruler. Her Divine Powers are represented on her head-dress by the feathers of the Celestial and Terrestrial Truth; the orb of the Sun; the two Goddesses ruling the commencement and the fruition, represented by the horned and orbed uræii, symbols of beauty, life, and fierce protective motherhood; the ram's horns of all-penetrating potency; the nemess with the fiery serpent of prophecy and protection upright before her face.

Above the figure of the Queen is the Mother-vulture; at once the avenging, protective, and intuitive emissary of MAUT the Mother of all things; holding the Seal composed of a ring and a plate engraved with the symbols of the birth-presiding forces which gave a name of power to the Queen.

Behind her is her KA or real Ego; the hands, lifted in aspiration above the head, enclose the rectangular parallelogram representing the Portal of Wisdom in which is written the HORUS or heroic Name which according to Egyptian dogma was to be won by the Theurgic rites of Initiation. On it is seated the Royal Horus Baie. In the hands of the Ka is the Staff or Magical Wand which, rightly understood, was a means of transmitting the Royal Power to such of her subjects as she selected to carry out her Will.

Proclus in *Timæus* book v., page 330 says, speaking of the Baie, Spirit:

" Her seeds are hurled into the realms of generation ; and she must purify herself from circumjacent fluctuations of matter. For she contains two-fold powers, one leading to generation the other from generation to true being. The one leads her round the Genesiurgic, the other round the intellectual circle."

In this way we come to the consideration of the magical Power of the Soul : called by the Egyptians the Yekh, Khou or Shining One. We find in nearly all the Magical Tales that it was through the initiative of the Khou that really magical acts were performed. M. Chabas in his supplement to the *Harris Magical Papyrus* gives many instances of the good and evil uses made of the Khou.

One entered the body of a princess who was obsessed for a long period, until it was cast out by means of the health-giving Divinity.

It was the Khou which had been degraded that became a demon and the torturer of mankind. The fate of such was to sacrifice the negatively evil, those who had neglected their opportunities ; but the evil Khous could not themselves be annihilated. An evil immortality awaited the great evil-doer or destroyer among mankind; just as a beautiful immortality awaited the Shining Ones who had added to the beauty of life in their mortal days. Between these extremes of beauty and destruction lay the impotent and the ignorant, whose blindness doomed them to annihilation.

The beatitude of the Justified Khou was by no means purely contemplative. The inscription on the obelisk of Queen Hatshepsu (sometimes spelled Hatshepset) speaks of them as holding converse with the ungenerated souls during the one hundred and twenty years that the latter circle round the Sun. They had the power to take all imaginable forms, or to move hither and thither as they pleased.

We find in the *Ritual of the Dead* elaborate formulas for the assistance of the KHOU of the deceased. The Justified KHOU was obliged to pass many tests; it had to cultivate the gardens of heaven, destroy monsters, take on certain obligatory forms, escort the Gods in their Heaven-traversing ships, take part in the ceaseless struggle between the two contending forces, cross burning and desolate zones, suffer in the regions of hunger, thirst, and terror, submit to proofs, reply to questions, and pass the armed and hideous Deity who guarded the Portals of Wisdom.

Now, if an Egyptian failed in standing such tests as these, in the ceremony of his initiation, he was regarded as a man liable to become an evil KHOU if his power was developed: and in their Wisdom the Priests rejected him and left him in that ignorance which led to oblivion and the annihilation of the incarnating Ego. Not only this, but if he, by underhand means, found out magical formulas and was able to use them effectively, the punishment was death.

Details of this kind are given in the supplement to M. Chabas' translation of the *Harris Magical Papyrus*. The period was that of Rameses III. Compare this quotation:

> "HAI, the evil man, was a shepherd. He had said:—
>
> "'Oh! that I might have a book of spells that would give me resistless power.'
>
> "He obtained a book of the Formulas of Rameses-Meri-Amen, the Great God, his royal Master. By the Divine Powers of these, he enchanted men. He obtained a deep vault furnished

with implements. He made waxen images of men, and love-charms. And then he perpetrated all the horrors that his heart conceived."

Now on the face of the matter it is very easy to see that a great part of Egyptian Magic lay in a species of Hypnotism, called by later magicians, Enchantment, Fascination, and so forth. Anybody with intelligence and charm can hypnotise an innocent person that interests him, but such a practice is derogatory both to fascinator and fascinated, even when it takes place in matters of ordinary passional life. How much more so when it leads to debauchery of the soul. In this way we perceive the possibility of an Uninitiate successfully performing the spells he had discovered.

Rituals or Ceremonies now simply regarded as a waste of time by those who have to assist at their celebration, had a potent effect when the symbolism of each action was fully recognised, and when the imagination was extended and ultra-sensitive, and the Will concentrated firmly and repeatedly, on the object to be accomplished. The KA of the Ritualist was thus at high tension acting upon its counterpart the concave germ in the AB (heart) or vessel of conscious desire; this reacts upon the HATI (Instinctive habit) or unconscious executant. The whole human Ego then being in a state of theurgic excitation the BAIE (spirit) descended and the whole being became a luminous KHOU or Shining Body of super-human potency, the Augoeides of the Greek Mystics.

This glittering being established in the midst of the SAHU (Elemental Body) then by its radiation can awake corresponding potencies in nature. For this purpose the KHAIBT was used as a link between the Ego and the non-Ego, and the spiritual body or ZET was established.

When this condition was brought about, a man became in the eyes of the Egyptians, Osirified. That is to say, a Microprosopus, or Perfect copy of the Macroprosopus. But he who, ignorant and unpurified, performed these rites, became the habitation of an illusive and fatal force, ever dragging him down to the deep abysses of blind potency.

We may now perceive dimly how the Egyptians conceived the seed of the Tree of Life-Eternal to be implanted in the heart of each man or woman born on earth; how it can wither and fade; how it can be cultivated until the man becomes either an Evil Demon or a God.

To the high initiate there was no question of choice in this matter. He knew that the heart turned inward on itself was a very poor alternative for that expansion of being that belongs to the development of the whole latent Divine Powers of the Microprosopus. In other words, the perfect formulation of the Osiris soul, the Holy Spirit of the Divine, made manifest and eternal.

Now the Egyptians had elaborated a marvellous system of symbolism. The forms of the universal powers or Gods, stood, each complete, behind a human or animal mask; his Divinity symbolized by his head-dress, his powers by his Staff and the Symbol of Life which he bore in his hands. MM. Chabas and Textor de Ravisi have told us that the most potent magical formula was the identification of the Ritualist with the God whose power he was invoking. So increasing himself to an immeasurable greatness he leapt beyond all bodies, and transcending time became eternity. He became higher than all height, lower than all depth. He knew himself part of the great chain of Creation at once unbegotten, young, old, dead. He felt within himself latent, unfolding faculties, and retained the memory of experiences gained in time long past and dead. His feet to-day stood in the place that yesterday his eye could scarcely see, and beyond him in the Invisible was his next day's resting place.

In the sixty-fourth chapter of the *Book of the Dead*, dating back to the IVth dynasty about 3733 B.C., the rubric tells us that:

"If this chapter is known the person is made triumphant upon earth, and in the nether world, and he performeth all things that are done by the living. This composition is a secret—not to be seen or looked at. Recite the chapter when sanctified and pure, not approaching women, not eating goats' flesh or fish."

The text contains the following passages:

"I am Yesterday, To-day and To-morrow, for I am born again and again. I am That Whose Force is unmanifest and nourisheth the Dwellers in the West. I am the Guider in the East. The Lord of the Two Faces Who seeth by His own Light. The Lord of Resurrections Who cometh forth from the Dusk and Whose Birth is from the House of Death.

"Ye Two Divine Hawks upon your stations; Watchers of the Material World; ye who go with the bier to its eternal home, and ye who conduct the Ship of the Sun; advancing onwards from the highest Heaven to the place of the Sarcophagus.

"This is the Lord of the Shrine which standeth in the centre of the Earth, He is in me; and I am in Him.

"Mine is the radiance in which PHTHA floateth over His Firmament.

"Oh! Sun Who smileth gladly, and whose heart is delighted with the perfect Order of this day as thou enterest into Heaven and comest forth in the East: the Ancients and those Who are gone before, acclaim thee!

"Let thy paths be made pleasant for me.

"Let thy ways be made wide for me to traverse the earth and the expanse of Heaven. Shine Thou upon me, O penetrating power, as I draw near to the Divine Words my ears shall hear in the Abodes of the West. Let no pollution of that which brought me forth be upon me. Deliver me, protect me from him who closeth His Eyes at twilight and bringeth to an end in darkness. (The annihilator.)

"I am He Who bursteth the Bonds. Uttermost Extension is my Name. I bring to its fulness the Force which is hidden within me.

. . . . .

"I am He Who cometh forth as One Who breaketh open the Gates: and Everlasting is the Daylight which His Will hath created. I know (have power over) the Deep Waters, is my Name.

. . . .

"I shine forth as the Lord of Life and the glorious Law of Light.

. . . . .

"I come as the Ambassador of the Lord of Lords to avenge the cause of Osiris in this Place. Let the Eye consume its tears. I am the Guide to the House of Him Who dwelleth in His Treasures.

. . . .

"I travel on high, I tread upon the Firmament, I raise a flame with the lightning which mine eye hath made, and I fly forward towards the Splendours of the Glorified in the presence of the Sun, who daily giveth Life to every man who walketh about the habitations of the earth.

"Oh! thou who leapest forth! Conductor of the Shades and the glorified Ones from the earth! Let the fair path to the Western Abodes, which is made in behalf of those who faint, and for the restoration of those who are in pain, be granted unto me.

"Blessed are they who see the bourne. Beautiful is the God of the motionless heart, who restoreth Peace to the Torrent.

"Behold! there cometh forth the Lord of Life, Osiris, Thy support who abideth day and night.

. . . . .

"I fly up to heaven and I alight upon earth and mine eye turneth back towards the traces of my footsteps. I am the offspring of yesterday. The caverns of the earth have given me birth, and I am revealed at my appointed time."

This is the Triumphant Death-Song of the Initiated Egyptian. To Him the Life beyond the grave—the abodes of the West—opened a wider range of activity. To him Initiation meant the hastening of the Time of Ripened Power when he might become One with the Great God of Humanity, Osiris; slain that he might rise again, perfected through suffering, glorified through humiliation.

This was the highest work of magic, the Spiritual Alchemy or the Transmutation from human Force to Divine Potency. As is said by the great Iamblichus, in section iv., chapter ii., of *The Mysteries:*

"The Priest who invokes is a man; but when he commands powers it is because through arcane symbols, he, in a certain respect, is invested with the sacred Form of the Gods."

Iamblichus also tells us that the daimon or elemental

ruler is received at the hour of birth. It is a personification of the Symbol imprinted on the SAHU or Elemental body; and its action may be defined as that of Fate or Destiny. Its forces are drawn from the whole world, and it is established in the SAHU before the soul descends into generation. He says further :

> " And when the soul has received Him as her leader the Daimon immediately presides over the soul, gives completion to its lives, and binds it to body when it descends. He likewise governs the common animal of the soul (the SAHU) and directs its peculiar life, and imparts to us the principles of all our thought and reasonings. We also perform such things as he suggests to our intellect, and he continues to govern us till, through sacerdotal theurgy, we obtain a God for the inspective guardian and leader of the soul. For then the Daimon either yields or delivers his government to a more excellent nature, or is subjected to him as contributing to his guardianship, or in some other way is ministrant to him as to his Lord."

When this takes place, and the body, sealed by destiny, is made subject, by initiation, to the Divine Powers, it may well be symbolised by the Ka supporting the Baie on the portal of initiation. The Lower Self being sacrificed to the Higher Self. The Osiris Man is established, as in the symbols in which the Osiris is represented by the TAT or Symbol of Stability. Then, and then only, is the question of Sacrifice for others to be considered. And the Osiris may plunge once again into matter ; once again making use of his mummied form to seek and to save that which was lost.

Mild saintliness was by no means the ideal of the Egyptian Priesthood. Intense practical interest in the life of their country, and the ennobling of natural functions, drew a sharp contrast between them and the ascetics of India and Christendom. "Whatever your hand findeth to do do it with your might," is a text that may well have come down to us from Ancient Egypt. The generative processes of Nature were honoured by them at special festivals—but at the same time the degradation of natural functions by excess was sternly reprimanded.

The Laws of Moses were to a great extent derived from the Laws of Ancient Egypt, and whatever else may be said of them they certainly tend to sanitary conditions, and length of life, individual and racial.

Now we know that with the Jews Magic was practised in the Sanctuary, but denounced by the Priesthood; it was only when Saul found the Sacred Oracles of the Urim and Thummim deaf to his questions that he consulted a mistress of the AUB or Astral Light.—1 Samuel xxviii. v. 7.

So in Egypt we find side by side with the high Theurgic mysteries (of which a good idea may be formed from the writings of Iamblichus), a more material development of Magical Art. At the Leyden Museum there is a large collection of magical formulæ of late date; but the best specimen now at hand is the hieratic Papyrus of Harris probably dating back to the XVIIIth Dynasty. It contains twenty-two formulas which may be divided into three parts; the first including Songs addressed to Shu, to the Five Great Gods of Hermopolis, and to Ammon-Ra, of which I here give a translation, as follows:

THE BOOK OF SONGS POWERFUL AGAINST THE INHABITANTS OF THE WATERS.

I.

HYMN TO SHU.

Hail to thee Child of Ra, First-born, Flesh of his Flesh. By Him hast thou been tried since thy birth. Valorous One, Lord of the Transformations, overthrowing the impious each day. At the Breath of Thy Mouth the Ship rejoices, the vessel is made glad: for they perceive Shu, Son of Ra, triumph over his enemies and strike the impure with his spear. He pilots the Sun to the heights of the Heavens from the dawning of each day. Tefnut rests upon his head. She darts out her flames against his enemies and behold they are not. Formed by Ra, endowed with greatness, inheritor of his father's Throne, His Powers expand and are one with the Powers of Ra.

II.

(The origin attributed to this papyrus is the usual source by which revelations were conveyed to the Egyptians.)

He (Shu) wrote this book for the library in which are the writings of the Lord of Hermopolis at the Southern Abode of Harmachus: in the Pylon of the Palace of Hermonthis. And he placed it sculptured and engraved under the feet of Ra Harmachus.

III.

HYMN TO SHU.

Hail to thee, Son of Ra, Begotten by Tmu, self-created without substance. Thou art the Very Lord of the twofold Truth. The Master Who commands the Gods. Thou guidest the sight of thy Father Ra. All honour unto thee who with thine own hands hast directed the inclinations of the Gods.

The furies of the great Goddess are calmed by Thee. By the Fire of His Will He draws forth His Strength and all the Gods fear His Face. He is King of the Heights and of the Depths of the Land of Shu, Son of Ra, Life Pure and Strong. The God of the morning of Time. Formed of the substance of the Sun in Hermon-this to overcome the enemies of his Father. Thou sailest peaceably in the bark, the boatmen are filled with joy. All the Gods Invoke Thee, and give thee praise when they hear Thy Name. Thou art more mysterious than the Gods, Thou art twice great in thy Name of Shu, Son of Ra.

IV.

Adjuration to the Crocodile.

Stop Crocodile.Mako, Son of Satem, I am An-Hur, Great Master of the sword.

Litany to Shu.

1. Greater and Vaster than the Gods art Thou in Thy Name of the Great Goddess.
2. Thy twofold plume out-tops the Heavens in Thy Name of the God Who raises up the Two-fold Plume.
3. Thou sustainest Thyself upon Thy Shield in Thy Name of the God that is established upon his shield.
4. From Thy Throne Thou guidest the Upper Heavens in thy name of An-Hur.
5. Thou destroyest the Storm, thou illuminatest the desolation in thy Name of the God Who destroyeth the Storm.
6. Thou exorcisest the Crocodile risen from the Abyss, in Thy Name of God Who exorciseth Crocodiles.

7. Thou hast thy spear which shall pierce the heads of the impious in Thy Name of the Horned God.

8. Thou smitest those who approach in thy Name of Smiting with the Double Horns.

9. Thy Forms are vaster than the Gods in thy Name of Chief God of the City of Tenu.

10. The Sun came forth when thou camest forth in thy Name of Shu son of Ra.

11. Thou seizest thy spear and attackest the impious in thy Name of Horus Tenu.

12. Thou destroyest the iniquity of the world on the earth in thy Name of the Dwelling place of the Sun.

13. Thou massacrest the Asiatics and the Sati, in thy Name of First-born child.

14. Thy Name is more powerful than the Gods in thy Name of God Seated in the centre of thy ship.

15. The Force of Youth given to thy nostrils extends to the limits of the Thebaid, in thy Name of First-born Child.

16. Thou strikest the heads of the impious in thy Name of Lord of the Sacrifices.

17. Thou makest the Bark to sail with a favourable Wind in Thy Name of the Goddess Maat.

18. Oh! being who has formulated his own body!

19. Oh! only Lord proceeding from Noun!

20. Oh! Divine substance self-created!

21. Oh! God Who has made the substance that is within Him!

22. Oh! God who has formulated His Father and made fertile His Mother!

V.

Hail to ye, oh! Five Great Gods, come from Hermopolis, ye who are not in heaven, who are not on earth, and who shine not in any light. Come to me. Test thou the river for me. Bind that which dwells therein. Let not that which swims, pass. Shut the mouths, shut the mouths, make fast the jaws, make fast the jaws.

As the sword is fixed in the scabbard when the earth is lightened from the east as the edge of the swords of the great Goddesses, ANATA and ASTATE are concealed. They conceive and bring not forth. They are sealed by the Gods. They have been created by Set. They are overcome by that which is above and which brings forth Good.

VI.

Adoration of Ammon Ra Harmachis, who created himself who possessed the earth from the beginning, composed by the Divine Cynocephali of the God Put-Api, in order to adore the Majesty of the August God Ammon-Put-To when he shines on the Noun which is the Goddess Nu. These words are to be said over water and earth.

Hail to Thee the Holy One Who hast formed thyself, Vast in Thy Measure, Illimitable, Divine Chief rejoicing in the power of creating himself. Vast and Flaming Serpents of Wisdom, Strength Supreme and Mysterious Form. Invisible Spirit. Author of His Unconquerable Power, King of the Higher and the Lower Land, Ammon Ra. Perfect and forceful Light. Created from Himself! Twofold Horizon. Hawk of the East. Brilliant. Illuminating. Blazing forth. Intelligence more intellectual than the Gods. Thou art hidden in the great Ammon. In thy transformation thou revolvest in the solar disk. God, Totnen, Vaster than the Gods. Thou wast old and art born again. Wanderer of the Centuries. Ammon eternal in all things. Thou, the God whose thought begat the World.

(Adjuration against all inhabitants of Water.) Come unto me Strong and vigorous Life of the Gods. Destroy the perils which surround me, from the plants which are in the waters. Let them be for me like pebbles upon the earth. Let the dangers disappear as hunger disappears in a fruitful land.

VII.

Hymn to Ammon-Ra, said by the Divine Cynocephali of the God Put-Api-To. In the great adoration of the God who is in the midst of the Waters, whose bones are of silver, and flesh of gold, and behind whose head is the true Lapis Lazuli.

The Divine Cynocephali say :

Oh Ammon hidden in the centre of his eye, spirit which shines in the sacred eye, adoration to the Holy Transformers, to those which are not known! brilliant are his forms veiled in a blaze of Light. Mystery of Mysteries, Concealed mystery ; Hail to thee in the midst of the heavens. Thou, who art Truth, hast brought forth the gods. The Signs of Truth are in thy mysterious sanctuary. By thee is thy mother Meron made to shine. Thou puttest forth illuminating rays. Thou surroundest the earth with thy light until thou returnest unto the mountain which is in the Country of Aker. Thou art adored in the waters. The fertile earth adores thee. When thy cortege passes to the hidden mountain the wild animal rises in his lair, the spirits of the east praise thee, they fear the light of thy disk. The spirits of the Khenac acclaim thee when thy Light shines in their faces. Thou traversest another heaven over which thine enemy may not pass. The fire of thy heat attacks the monster Ha-her. The fish Teshtu guard the waters around thy bark. Thou orderest the dwelling of the monster Oun-ti, which Nub-ti strikes with his sword. This is the God who seized the heaven and the earth in his tempest. His virtue is powerful to destroy his enemy. His spear is the instrument of death for the monster Oubn-ro. Suddenly seizing him he holds him down ; he makes himself master of him and forces him to re-enter his abode ; then he devours his eyes and therein is his triumph ; then is the monster devoured by a burning flame ; from the head to the feet all his members burn in its heat. Thou bringest thy servants to the haven with a favourable wind. Under thee, the winds find peace. Thy bark rejoices, thy paths are enlarged, because thou hast overcome the ways of the author of evil.

Sail, wandering stars! Sail on shining stars; ye who wander with the winds! For thou art resting in the bosom of the sky, thy mother embraces thee; when thou comest unto the western horizon, the earth holds up his arms to receive thee. Thou who art worshipped by all existing things!

Adjuration against Lions, Crocodiles and Reptiles.

Come unto me, oh Lord of the Gods! Make the lions of Meru to depart. The crocodiles going up from the river and the sting of the venomous reptiles creeping from their holes! Stop Mako, Crocodile, Son of Set! Swim not, use not thy limbs, open not thy jaws! May the water become an ardent fire before thee, thou whom the Thirty Seven Gods have formed. Who wast bound by the great serpent of the Sun and who wast bound with great chains of metal before the bark of Ra. Protect me, Ammon, fertilizer of the substance of thy being.

Say this over an image of Ammon in the form of the God with Four Rams' Heads, painted on a plaque of white clay, a crocodile under his feet, divine cynocephali making adoration on the right hand and on the left.

The second part of this papyrus consists of formulas to enchant and protect the reciter from water monsters. In all these the great formula of protection is the Assumption of the Form of some God; Khem, Shu, or Anubis as the case may be.

It would appear that the crocodile held in Ancient Egypt the same position as the Dweller of the Threshold did in the mind of the author of *Zanoni*. Something terrible was to assail those who ventured into the fluidic realms of the invisible; the Nile and the crocodiles therein are the symbols of the River of Phantasy full of delusions that must be traversed by the aspiring Soul.

The last three chapters of the Harris papyrus contain interesting formulæ. One is a Ritual of Banishment to be performed in the South, North, West, and East, with the formulation of a guardian in the shape of a dog that was to be terrible to all attacking forces. The translation is as follows:

"Arise, Dog of Evil, that I may instruct thee in thy present duties. Thou art imprisoned. Confess thou that it is so. Horus it is who has given this commandment. Let thy face be terrible as the storm-parted sky. Let thy jaws close pitilessly. Make sacrifice as the God Her-Shafi. Massacre as the Goddess Anata. May thy hair stand up like rods of fire. Be thou great as Horus and terrible as Set. Equally to the South, to the North, to the West and to the East. The whole land belongs unto thee. Nothing shall stop thee, while thou settest thy face in my defence; while thou settest thy face against savage beasts; while thou settest thy face to protect my paths, opposing thyself to the enemy. I bestow upon thee the power of banishing, of becoming noiseless and invisible. For thou art my guardian, courageous and terrible."

The next formula is similar, but specifies exactly the dangers feared by a sleeper, which are to be guarded against by the Watcher.

The last formula is a list of names, of which no explanation is offered by M. Chabas, and regarding which we may bear in mind the injunction, "Change not barbarous names of evocation."*

Baron Textor de Ravisi on page 286 of the *Memoir of the Congress of French Orientalists* held at St. Etienne, 1875, defines the different kinds of supernatural apparitions described by the Egyptians.

"Before the entire resurrection of the body," he says,

* See *Chaldean Oracles*, edited by Wynn Westcott, page 47.

"the justified KA could, if it chose, re-animate the body of the dead. Such apparitions usually menace some evil doer, give injunctions, or predict death."

Such be it remembered would be also the constitution of the vampire, when the corpse is said to be found fresh as the day when it was laid in its tomb. Ravisi defines manifestations which are visible but intangible; of which the head is distinctly seen, but of which the limbs are vaporous, to be composed of the KA and the ZET. Their nature is sweet and consolatory. The manifestations which resemble the bodily form of the deceased, but are intangible, are composed of the KA and the SAHU. They are generally terrifying. Manifestations of the AB and the HATI re-united in the ZET (Spiritual body) are only visible to the spiritual senses. Manifestations of the image of the mortal procured through a medium are due to the KHAIBT alone, and have none of the individuality of the KA in them.

An initiated King received four names; the second of which was the KA name. Now to know the secret name or REN of a man meant in the eyes of the Egyptians the knowledge of the most powerful means of influencing that man; it could be used as a means of exercising his personal qualities through the power of his name. We know that the Jews never called their God by His Name except for some sacred purpose, and this was probably a tradition derived from Egypt through Moses.

The greatest merit was attributed to the Son who made his father's name to live; for this meant that the Dead man's KA survived, was invoked, received offerings, and heard his glory or his virtues sung by his successors.

Now we find in the following legend that the "Ren" or True Name was a secret to be gained by those who wished for the knowledge of the most powerful formulæ, just as in Christian belief the *Word* is the Child of God, the Manifestor of Life Eternal, and at the name of Jesus every knee must bow.

THE LEGEND OF RA AND ISIS.

Date XXth Dynasty.

Now Isis was a Woman knowing Words of Magical Power, her heart was weary of multitudes of men, and she chose the multitude of Gods, but above all the multitude of the Shining Ones. And she meditated in her heart and said " Might not I, also, by means of the names of Shining Power become as the Sun God in Heaven ? "

Now Ra and His Cycle of Powers were established every day in the Abodes of the Horizon. Ancient was the Divine One and his Mouth dropped forth water. The water fell upon the earth, dew from his lips fell upon the ground. Isis kneaded this with the earth, and made it in the form of a serpent of power divine and in the image of a dart. She placed it not before her forehead, but left it lying in the path that the will of the great God had placed between his two domains. The God of Power crowned and holy was followed by the Gods of the twofold abodes life, strength and health.

Now Ra proceeded as was his daily wont.

Its being shone forth from the sacred serpent ; the fire of life shot from its body, and the dweller among the cedars was prostrated. Then Ra the God of gods opened his mouth, and the cry of his might, life, strength, and well-being reached up to heaven. The Company of Gods cried out : " What is it ? " and again the Gods said " What is it ? " But Ra found no voice with which to answer. His teeth chattered, his limbs trembled, the poison flowed through his veins, as the Nile God flows in his course. Then the might of the God confirmed his will and he cried out to those in his train :

" Come unto me, ye who proceeded from me. Ye powers that came forth from me let the Creative Form be told that I am wounded by a deadly thing. My heart knoweth it. Mine eyes have not seen it. My hand hath not fashioned it. I know not who hath made this thing. I have not tasted pain like unto it. No pain is like unto it. I am a prince, son of a prince created by a god. I am the Mighty Son of the Mighty, Strength of my Father is my name. I am of many names and of many forms, the Divine Image of my Being is in every god. I have been heralded by Tmu and Horus, the formulators of the Formless. My Father and Mother gave me my name as an infant, it was concealed in my body so that the enchanter might not gain power over me by his enchantments. I had come forth from my abode to see the world I had fashioned, and was passing over my creation when I was stricken by I know not what. Is it Fire? Is it Water? My heart is full of Fire, my limbs tremble, my flesh is seized as with an ague.

" I pray you let my divine offspring be brought to me. Light is in their Words, Wisdom is in their mouths, their powers reach unto heaven."

His cries brought his divine children unto him. Isis came with her words of Light; the Breath of Life was in her mouth; and her disease-destroying incantations, her words giving life to silent hearts. She said:

"Oh! Divine Father, what is this? What is it? A serpent hath made thee fear, one of thy darts hath lifted up its head against thee, it shall be overthrown by words of beneficent power. I will make it depart from the sight of thine eyes."

The holy God opened his mouth, saying:

"I was passing along the path which divideth my twofold dominion, wishing in my heart to behold my creation. I was stung by a serpent, I saw it not. Is it Fire? Is it Water? I am colder than Water, I am hotter than Fire. My limbs sweat. I tremble. My eye dims. I cannot see the heaven; sweat rises on my face as in the time of sorrow."

Said Isis unto Ra:

"Oh tell me thy name, oh my divine Father, for Life is in the Power of thy name."

Said RA:

"I am the maker of heaven and earth, supporting the mountains, creating what existeth thereon. I am the maker of water, bringing forth the floods, making fruitful the Universe, giving increase. I am the Maker of Heaven and have made beautiful the horizon. I have given the spirit of the Gods a place therein. I am he, who when he openeth his eyes, bringeth forth light, and when he closeth his eyes, bringeth forth darkness. I am the Nile God whose name the Gods know not, bringing about the inundation with my word. I am the Maker of hours, the Creator of days. I am the opener of the yearly festival, the creator of rushing water, the maker of living fire. I cause the abodes of delight to be built. I am Kephera in the darkness, Ra in the midday, and Tmu in the evening."

But the poison was not driven out of its course, the great God found no peace; so Isis said unto RA:

"Thou hast not told me thy name. Oh, tell it unto me and the poison shall depart, for life is in the Power of thy name."

The poison burned with burnings, it was stronger than flames of fire; the majesty of RA spake and said:

"I give myself to be searched out by Isis, my name shall pass from my body into her body."

The Divine One was hidden from the Gods, wide (void) was his seat in the Ship of millions of years. When the time had come for the passing forth of his heart she said unto her son Horus:

"Let him swear by the Divine Life to give unto me his divine eyes."

Thus was taken the name of the Great God. Isis the Mighty One of Enchantments said:

"Depart Poison. Pass forth from RA. Oh, Eye of Horus, come forth from the God and shine without his mouth. I, even I, have worked. I banish the poison to be dispersed upon the earth. It hath been overcome. Verily the name of the Great God hath been taken from him. May RA Live. May the poison die. May the poison die and may RA live. May Main son of Mainthe live. May the Poison die."

Thus said the Mighty Isis, Mistress of the Gods, who knew RA by his own name.

Such is the Legend of RA and Isis. Its incidents are known to us in the old tale of Merlin and the Witch Vivien. It is obviously a sun-myth, being, of course, an allegory of an eclipse of the Sun. In ancient symbolism the head and tail of a Dragon or Serpent represented the places of Solar and Lunar eclipse in the Zodiac. It is well known that the moment of eclipse has ever been felt to be fraught with sinister occult power.

Of the name of RA it is interesting to learn that he is credited with no less than seven BAIES and FOURTEEN KAS, each with its own name, corresponding to different attributes such as, Wealth, stability, majesty, glory, might, victory, and so forth, similar to the Qabalistic Sephiroth, or Emanations of Deity.

Each man's KA could at the death of the body enter into any image or picture or magical implement prepared for its reception. In the "Story of Setna," a demotic papyrus now in the Ghizeh Museum, and translated by Professor Flinders Petrie, in his second series of Egyptian tales, it is written:

> "Now in the Tomb was Na-Nefer-Ka-Ptah and with him was the KA of his wife Ahura, for though she was buried at Koptos, her KA dwelt at Memphis with her husband whom she loved."

That is to say it dwelt in a statue prepared for its reception. Now it seems exceedingly probable that as the mummy was the material basis for the SAHU and

KHAIBT, so the mummy-case with its painted presentment of the living person was the material basis for the preservation of the KA of a low grade initiate or the KHU of a fully-equipped Adept.

I append some quotations from the *Book of the Dead* in which the various parts of the human being are specially mentioned.

CHAPTER XXX.

AB of mine which is that of my mother. HATI of my coming into being. Thou art my KA (Ego), who art in my KHAT (Body). The artist who formeth and stengtheneth my limbs.

CHAPTER XXVI.

I know my AB (Will) I have gained power over my HATI (Instincts); I have gained power to do what pleaseth my KA (Ego).

CHAPTER LXXXIX.

A Prayer to Annitu that the BAIE (Spirit) may be reunited to the KHAT (Body).

Behold! Grant that the BAIE (Spirit) of Osiris may come forth. May he see his KHAT (Material Body); may he rest upon his SAHU (Astral form); May his ZET (Spiritual Body) never be destroyed.

CHAPTER XCI.

Is an Address to the Spirit of Spirits saying:

He maketh a Path for the Khou (Illuminated One) for the BAIE (Spirit) of Osiris. . . . I am furnished forth (or enrobed, armed). I am an armed KHOU, I have made my way to the place where Ra and Hathor dwell.

CHAPTER XCII.

The Path of BAIU (Spirits) is opened. My soul seeth it. The Great God within the Boat of Ra, the Light of

Souls, is my Soul. Let not my BAIE be imprisoned. Let not my KHAIBT be enchained. Let Paths be opened for my BAIE and my KHAIBT (Radiation). . . . Thy AB is with thee.

CHAPTER XLVI.

O ye recent offspring of Shu, who is possessor of his diadem at sunrise, dawn after dawn; oh ye future generations of men. (This Chapter is addressed to the Unborn Ones or Hammemit.)

Professor Flinders Petrie gives several instances of Magical practices in the Egyptian tales translated by him. In the first one dating from the fourth dynasty, Uba-Aner said:

"Bring me my casket of ebony and electrum." Whereupon he fashioned a crocodile of wax, seven fingers long. When cast in the water it became seven cubits long, swallowed the enemy and eventually disappeared on receiving permission to do so.

In *Baufra's Tale* the chief reciter spake his magic words and divided the waters; having found what he desired he spake again and the waters returned to their place.

In *Hordedef's Tale* the description of a magician is given:

"He eats five hundred loaves of bread and a side of beef, and drinks a hundred draughts of beer unto this day! He knows how to restore the head that is smitten off. He knows how to cause the lion to follow him, trailing his halter upon the ground. He knows the designs of the Abodes of Thoth. The majesty of Upper and Lower Egypt has long sought for the Designs of the Abodes of Thoth in order that he might have them copied on the Walls of his Pyramid. (There is an alternative suggestion that this may mean his horoscope.) For the magical ceremony the old magician required his books, and the assistance of his youths. The king asked him if he knew the number of the designs of the Abodes of Thoth. He replied, ' I know not their number, but I know where they are.' ' Where is that ? ' ' In a chest of whetstone in a chamber named the plan-room in Heliopolis and they are kept in this chest.' " A search was instituted, but the last part of the papyrus recording the details, is missing.

In the *Story of Bata* self-mutilation enabled him to draw out his HATI (Human heredity) and place it on the topmost flower of an acacia tree, so that he could not be killed unless the tree were cut down. When this happened his HATI was found in a seed; which, being placed in a cup of water grew, and his body reviving, he drank the water. Then he changed into a sacred Bull, which was eventually sacrificed; two drops of its blood fell upon the ground, these contained the HATI of Bata. They grew into a couple of persea trees, these were cut down, but a shaving from one of them was swallowed by his faithless wife, and she brought forth a child, in which Bata was reincarnated.

In the *Story of Ahura*, the Book of Thoth is described as follows :—" He wrote it with his own hands and it will bring a man to the Gods. To read two pages enables you to enchant the heaven, the earth, the abyss, the mountains and the sea; you shall know what the birds of the sky and the crawling things are saying; you shall see the fishes of the deep, for a divine power is there to bring them out of the depth. And when the second page is read, if you are in the world of ghosts, you will grow again in the shape you were on earth. You will see the sun shining in the sky, with all the gods, and the full moon." The book was concealed in the middle of the river at Koptos, in an iron box; with inner enclosing boxes of bronze, sycamore, ivory and ebony, silver and gold, and it was guarded by snakes and scorpions. Where the book was, there was light. When it was taken away, darkness reigned.

A funeral stele quoted in the *Harris Magical Papyrus*,

page 167, gives the history of a princess reported to be obsessed by a KHOU. The royal scribe has not power enough to drive out this evil demon. The God Chons finally delivered her. The God performed a health-giving ceremony and the KHOU retired peaceably, but was not deprived of its inherent faculty of occupying another body at pleasure. The same story informs us that in the Holy Place of the Temples secret books were kept (under the charge of special agents) which the Pharaoh consulted when in difficulties. M. Chabas gathers that the living might come to the help of the KHOU in its life beyond the tomb, by means of mystical formulæ pronounced under favourable circumstances, and with amulets or symbolic figures. The KHOUS on their side could manifest to the living, they could haunt or obsess a human being, and the living could only defend themselves with the aid of formulas, talismans or divine images.

In a papyrus before alluded to and quoted by M. Chabas, Hai the Shepherd obtained the book of magical formulas belonging to his royal master, and he managed by the process called "Neter Paut" or joining himself to a God Form, to procure the power of enchanting or fascinating men. He made images of Menh, which may mean wax or some more occult preparation. He made charms and telesmas to provoke love. He practised these things really and made them all to the horror of the Divine Ones. He paralysed a man's hand, and by means of a slave did things which the King did not allow even the Master of His house to perform. "He spoke, and said such and such a thing should be produced, he operated, and it was produced."

Here we have vague hints of possible magical formulas, but we must come down to much later times to find the relics of the more practical written details of magic as practised by the Ancient Egyptians. For of old they were carefully preserved from the profane.

There is, however, a fragment taken from a papyrus

preserved in the British Museum, No. XLVI (Greek), and there is also in the Leyden Museum a demotic papyrus with a Greek version, of which Leemans gives the following summary of contents:—
1. Magical ceremonies, performed by means of love considered as a great thaumaturgic power.
2. Receipt for a remedy ; by one Hermerius.
3. Receipt for happiness and good fortune.
4. Receipt by Agathodes, to produce a dream.
5. Receipt to procure a dream.
6. Receipt to preserve a dream.
7. Receipt for consulting a Deity.
8. Receipt for checking a man's anger.
9. Invocation of a Deity.
10. Receipt to procure dreams.
11 and 12. Receipt to procure rust upon gold.
13. To make a ring having the property of making every enterprise succeed, and of bringing good fortune.
14. Description of a similar ring.
15. The sphere of Democritus for prognosticating by calculation the recovery or death of a sick person.
16. A means of separation : a formula to cause separation between husband and wife, or other persons.
17. Formula for causing sleepless nights to a person until he dies. This section is embellished with a drawing of an Egyptian Deity.
18. A charm to make oneself beloved, and always have friends.
19. Explanations of certain mystical names of plants and other objects.

These works which appear to have been found at Thebes are attributed by Reuvens to some gnostic of the Marcosian school of the Third or Fourth Century of our era.

Professor Goodwin says that the magicians of this

period invoked by the powers of Moses, the God of Abraham, the Gods of Egypt, Persia, and Greece. They identify Gods and Daimons of all known myths. Their fundamental ideas seem to be derived from the old Egyptian religion, and he considers that the authors of these papyri may have been priests of Isis or Serapis, practising the particular kind of theurgy criticised by Porphyry, and defended by Iamblichus, who writing in reply to Porphyry says :—that he considers the world to be under the care of a host of daimons, who superintend the operations of nature, and that the priest or magician, duly initiated, becomes incorporated with the Divine and over-ruling powers of the Universe, so as to acquire a certain authority over these subordinate ministers. He mentions that the Chaldean magicians, whose invocations are addressed to the Gods alone, used no threats ; while the Egyptians occasionally do so, but only towards the Daimons. With regard to the formulæ he says that the Egyptians and Assyrians being sacred nations, a peculiar sanctity is attached to their languages which make them an appropriate medium for communication with the Deity. He also says that the Divine Names in use among these peoples having been handed down from remote antiquity, and preserved inviolate and immutable, have therefore a peculiar affinity with the immutable Gods.

The Egyptians invented and carried out unquestionably the best working system of national life as national life ever yet formulated. The power and duration of their civilisation prove this beyond doubt. The glory of their nation continued very nearly five times as long as the glory of any other nation excepting only that of the persistent Chinese. The science of Egypt was Applied Science, in the strictest sense of the word. No vague dreamings found a part in their metaphysics. For physics and metaphysics alike were made use of. Every department of thought, idea and imagination were as clearly mapped out in the minds of an initiated

Egyptian, as were the nomes (divisions) and towns of his own country. What is more, exact correspondences were as far as possible established between his country, his body, his soul, his mind, and the realms of idea, creation and formulation.

The Ancient Egyptian did not adopt the extreme doctrine of original sin, but certainly did not consider that all men were born free and equal. As far as can be ascertained there was no strict system of caste among the Egyptians; an aristocracy governed, but each individual of that aristocracy had to submit to such severe physical, intellectual and spiritual tests that only great natures could pass through them. A system of consecration and purification of a very real and very practical nature was the path to distinction among the elect of Ancient Egypt. The Egyptians of the time of Iamblichus blame their forefathers for the materiality of their religion; but its very materiality made it so much the more potent. Religion was a real force when it had behind it an initiated king and an adept priesthood.

The Pharaoh united in himself the powers of the North and of the South; of the Delta and the Said; of the Red Crown and the White Crown; of the Papyrus and the Lotus; of Horus and of Set; and of Ptah and of Ammon. Maspero gives on the 46th page of his book on Egypt the following address to the King, which no doubt acted by a species of Hypnotic suggestion and tended to exalt the Kinghood of the King when recited by the faithful :—

"Thou resemblest RA in all that thou doest. Therefore the wishes of thy heart are always fulfilled. If thou desirest a thing during the night, at dawn it is already there. If thou sayest, Come up on the mountains, the celestial water shall flow at thy word. For thou art RA incarnate and Khephera created in the flesh. Thou art the living Image of thy Father, Tmu; and Lord of the City of the Sun. The God who commands is in thy mouth. The God of Wisdom is in thy heart; thy tongue is the sanctuary of truth, a God sits upon thy lips, thy words are accomplished every day, and the wish of thy heart realises itself like that of Phtha when he creates his works. Since thou art eternal, everything acts according to thy designs and everything obeys thy words."

Again we have the following *Salutation to Pharaoh awakened*.

" Turn thy face to me oh rising sun, which lighteneth the world with thy beauty, disk sparkling amongst men that drivest away the darkness of Egypt. Thou resemblest thy father when he rises in heaven, and thy rays penetrate into all parts of the earth. There is no place deprived of thy beauty, for thy words rule the destinies of all lands. When thou art resting in thy palace, thou hearest all that is said in every country, for thou hast millions of ears. Thine eye is more brilliant than any star in heaven, and more piercing than the sun; if any one speak, even if the mouth that speaketh be within the walls of a house, its words reach thine ear. If any hidden action be committed thine eye perceives it. O! King gracious Lord, who givest to all the breath of life."

I now quote the following hymn to give some idea of the attributes assigned to the Great Gods.

Hymn to Phtha-Tanen.

" Hail to thee, oh Phtha-tanen, great God who concealeth his form . . . thou art watching when at rest, the father of all fathers, and of all gods . . . watcher who traversest the endless ages of eternity; the heaven was uncreated, uncreated was the earth, the water flowed not; thou hast formulated the earth, thou hast united thy limbs, thou hast counted thy members. What thou hast found apart thou hast put into its place. Oh! God, Architect of the World, Thou art without a Father, Begotten by thine Own Growth;

Thou art without a Mother, being born by reflection of thyself. Thou drivest away the darkness by the beams of thine Eyes. Thou ascendest into the Zenith of Heaven; and thou comest down even as thou wentest up. When Thou art a dweller in the Infernal World, Thy knees are above the earth, and Thy Head is in the Upper Sky, Thou sustainest the substances which thou hast made. It is by thine own strength that thou movest; Thou art raised up by the might of thine own arms, thou weighest upon thyself kept firm by the mystery which is in thee. The roaring of thy voice is in the clouds; thy breath is on the mountain tops; the waters of thy inundation cover the lofty trees of every region . . Heaven and earth obey the command which thou hast given . . . Thou restest and it is Night; when thine Eyes shine forth we are illuminated; Oh! let us give glory to the God Who hast raised up the sky, and who causest his disk to float over the bosom of Mut. Who hath made Gods and men and all their generations. . . Thou the babe who is brought forth daily. Oh thou Ancient One Who has reached the limits of Time; Thou Immovable One Who traverseth every Path; the Height which cannot be attained."

THE GNOSTIC MAGIC OF EGYPT.

Having given quotations which illustrate the various aspects of Magic as it was taught and practised at the best period of Ancient Egypt, we may now pass on to the consideration of the later forms of the higher magic existing in Alexandria during the second and third centuries of our era. Mr. G. R. S. Mead has given us a translation of the *Pistis Sophia* which is regarded as the most precious and perfect relic of the followers of the *Gnosis;* as this volume is now in circulation I shall not allude to it further; but I propose to give considerable extracts from a Coptic papyrus of much the same date, which was found by Mr. Bruce in Upper Egypt: it has never before been translated into English.

The magical words and formulæ of this papyrus give some idea of the kind of sounds understood by initiates to be concealed under such symbols as the "I H V H" of the Hebrews, and the Hieroglyphic word groups of the Egyptians. Unfortunately we can never discover the secrets of the Egyptian vowels through the study of Hieroglyphs for the consonants alone are noted, as in Hebrew; and no system analogous to pointing was adopted by the later Egyptians. It is only then in the study of Coptic papyri that we can hope to discover some traces of the real ancient pronunciation of Magical Names.

This Coptic text resembles the dialect of the Said. Woïde the original transcriber declares the origin of the papyrus to be Theban. But M. E. Amelineau considers that the original work was written in Greek. The date is probably the second or third century of our era. Basilides and Valentinus, the two greatest Egyptian Gnostics, did all they could to gain adherents in Egypt and probably produced several works of the kind. I have given a translation of the most interesting parts of the papyrus, and will here remark that the greater part of it consists of Sigils, Keys and numbers, and the names of watchers and guardians, which at once remind the student of the *Book of the Dead*, notably of the eighteenth chapter in which the formulas of the various localities have to be known; also of the hundred and forty-sixth chapter treating of the twenty-one Pylons (gates) with their guardians and watchers; and, finally, of the hundred and forty-seventh chapter giving the names of the door-keepers, the watchers, and the heralds.

In these portions we have a distinct analogy with the Egyptian Esoteric Methods of Initiation. But the present ignorance of the real way in which to use "Secret Formulæ" makes these portions of ancient Gnostic tracts uninteresting to the generality of occult students. For this reason one formula only will be given as an example; this specimen is general in its nature, but it is one of which it was said that "if performed with arcane knowledge, it would suffice to open all the gates, unto which the soul could aspire."

Let us first, however, consider the essential principles of Gnosticism, which are briefly as follows:—

First—A denial of the dogma of a personal supreme God, and the assertion of a Supreme Divine Essence, consisting of the purest Light, and pervading that boundless space of perfected matter which the Greeks called the Pleroma. This Light called into existence the Great Father and the Great Mother whose children were the Æons or God-spirits. That is to say from the Supreme issues the *Nous* or Divine Mind; and thence successive emanations, each less sublime than the preceding. The Divine Life in each becoming less intense until the boundary of the Pleroma, or the Fulness of God is reached. From thence there comes into being a taint of imperfection, an abortive and defective evolution, the source of materiality and the origin of a created universe, illuminated by the Divine, but far removed from its infinitude and perfection. (The Little Thought of the text quoted below.)

Now the Gnostics considered that the actual ruler and fashioner of this created universe and its beings good and evil, was the Demiurgos, a power issuant from Sophia or Wisdom. By some it was said that the desire of souls for progression caused the origin of a Universe in which they might evolve and rise to the divine.

The Gnostics definitely believed in the theory of Cycles of Ascent and return in the evolutionary progress of worlds, ages, and man; the ascents and descents of the soul; the pre-existence of all human souls now in worldly life and the surety that all souls that desire the highest must descend to matter and be born of it. They were the Philosophical Christians.

The Rule of the Christian Church however fell into the hands of those who encouraged an emotional religion, destitute of philosophy; whose members should be bound together by personal ties of human sympathy with an exalted sufferer and preacher, rather than by an intellectual acceptance of high truth.

The Gnostics dissented from the creed then being defined, on the ground of the inferiority of the Hero worship of Christ, to the spiritual knowledge of the supernal mind, which they considered He taught.

The Gnostics were almost universally deeply imbued with the doctrines of Socrates and Plato; and a religion of emotion and reverence, combined with moral platitudes, did not seem to them of a sublimity sufficiently intense to be worthy to replace the Religious Mysteries of Egypt, India, and Persia, the Theocracy of the Jews, or the sublime truths hidden in the myths of Greece.

The Gnostic doctors were men who before all had received Hellenic culture. Their systems prove that they knew the works of the philosophers and had united them with the purely oriental ideas flowing from the ancient religions of Egypt, Chaldea, Persia and India. Their aim was to amalgamate the ideas of the East and the Philosophy of the Greeks with the inborn potency of the Christian faith.

The important formulas of the Three Baptisms I have given in full, so that the student may observe the link they create between the Magical Ceremonies of Initiation and the sacraments of the Roman and especially the Greek Christian Church. For in the ceremonies of the Greek Church there is an even closer adherence to the formulas of ancient wisdom than is found in the Roman Church.

A chart of the Pleroma is given by Valentinus, which may be described as follows:

First, is the Point, the Monad. (The Great Deep.)

Then the Triangle, the union of the point with the line. (The great Deep, Mind, and Truth.)

Then the Square, two vertical and two horizontal lines. (The Word, The Life, Man and the Assembly.)

Finally, the Pentagram and Hexad which with their reflected emanations count as ten and twelve, these together form the twenty-eight emanations or ideas of the Divine mind.

The Pleroma is bounded by a circumference emanating from the point or Monad, this is called the Horus or boundary, Stauros or cross, and Metæcheus or participator.

Without this circumference is the emanation of the "Sophia" sometimes called the "abortion," sometimes as in our text the "Little Thought," which is the universe as we know it.

I will end this introduction with one quotation from the *Pistis Sophia*:

"The spirit of the Saviour was moved in him,

and he cried, 'How long shall I bear with you? how long shall I suffer you? Do ye still not know, and are ye ignorant? Know ye not and do ye not understand, that ye are all Angels, and all Archangels, and Gods and Lords, and all Rulers. . . . That ye are from all; of yourselves and in yourselves in turn, from one mass, and one matter, and one essence.'"

Extracts from the Gnostic Papyrus.

(*Discovered by Bruce, and Preserved in the Bodleian Library.*)

The words in italics commencing each paragraph are merely a short summary of the contents.

The Book of the Knowledge of the Invisible.—Jesus, Lord of Life, He Who knoweth the Truth, spake and said: "I have loved you, I have desired Life for you."

This is the Book of the knowledge of the Divine Invisibility, according to the mystery hidden in the Book which guides the chosen people, hidden in the Peace of the Life of the Father, by means of the Saviour. He bought the souls that can receive this Word of Life, risen above all Life, by the knowledge of Jesus, Lord of life. He descended from His Father in the Æon of Light, in the fulness of the Pleroma (Perfect Nature), in the Knowledge which is the only real being, and which Jesus taught to His Apostles, saying:

"I give thee the Wisdom in which is contained all knowledge."

Jesus, Lord of Life, spake and said to His Disciples:

"Happy are those who crucify the World, and whom the world hath not crucified."

The Apostles replied to Him with one voice, saying:—

"Teach us how we may crucify the world, to the end that it shall not crucify us; that we shall neither be lost nor our lives wasted away."

Jesus, the Lord of Life, answered them and said :—
"He who crucifies the world is he who keeps my word, who fulfils the Will of Him who has sent me."

The Apostles answered unto him and said:—
"Speak, Lord, so that we may hear Thee. We have followed Thee with our whole hearts; we have left father, mother, pastures, and fields; we have abandoned riches and royal greatness, we have followed Thee that Thou mightest teach us the Life of the Father who has sent Thee."

Jesus, the Lord of Life, replied and said :—
"The Life of my Father is this, that you should receive the gift of the Spirit, that your souls should cease to be weighed down, by means of that which I am about to say to you, to the end that you may fulfil my Word and be saved from the Arkhon (Ruler) of this Aeon and his eternal illusion. But you, you my Disciples, hasten to receive my Words with a firm belief, treasure them in your hearts so that the Arkhon of the Æon, he who has no part in me, may not overcome you, so that you also, oh! my Apostles, may accomplish my words, through me. It is I Who have made you free to the end that you may live in holy liberty in which there shall be no stain; and as the Paraclete (Holy Spirit) has been purified, so may you also be sanctified through the Paraclete."

All the Apostles, Matthew and John, Philip, Bartholomew, and James replied with one voice :—
"Oh, Jesus, Lord of Life, from whom virtue floweth upon those who have obtained Thy Wisdom and Thy Likeness, who illuminatest by Thyself Light which is in the Light, which hath illuminated our hearts so that we can receive the Light of Life; the Word of Truth; which, by the Understanding, teacheth us all the knowledge hidden in the Lord of Life!"

Jesus, the Lord of Life said:
"Happy is the man who has known these things, who has brought down Heaven unto the Earth, who

has taken the Earth and raised it to the Heavens, so that they are no longer divided!"

The Apostles replied and said:

"Jesus, Lord of Life, tell us how we can make the Heavens to descend, for we have followed Thee in order that Thou mayest show us the Light of Truth."

Jesus, the Lord of Life, answered and said:

Of the Invisible Word.—"The Word was in Heaven before the Cosmos existed. If you know my Word you may make Heaven descend upon Earth, so that it may abide in you. Heaven is the Invisible Word of the Father; if you know it you have the Power to bring it down unto you. As to the Earth, I will show you how you may raise it unto Heaven, for the Earth which rises to Heaven is that which hears the Word of Wisdom, which has ceased to be a terrestrial spirit and has become celestial." . . .

Of the Image of the Pleroma. The Monad, or point.— The Image of the Pleroma is that in which we live and die. It is the Abode of the Father, the Garment of the Son, and the Strength of the Mother. It is the first Father of all things; it is the First Eternal One; it is the King of those whom no man can approach; it is that in which all things are lost; it is that which hath in Itself the form of all things; it is the abode which knoweth itself, which is born from itself; it is the abyss of all things; it is the greatness and truth which is in the abyss; it is that which gave birth to the Pleroma and which died for it. They have given it no name, for it is unnameable. The first source, which, in the future, shall be in all places. The First Sound comprehending all sounds that shall ever be heard. It is that of which the members form countless myriads of Powers, each contained in each.

Of the Father, the Demiurgus, the Creative God. The Line, or duad.—The Second Abode is that which is called the Demiurgus, Father, Word, Source, Nous, Man, Eternal, Infinite. It is the Column; it is the

Watcher; it is the Father of all things; it is He on Whose head the Æons form a radiant Crown; the Exterior Worlds cannot tell the Fulness of His Countenance; they are ever seeking its Light; because His Word has reached them, they desire to see Him. The Light of His Eyes penetrates the abodes of the Exterior Pleroma, and His Word goes forth from His Mouth; it reaches both those who inhabit the Heavens, and those who dwell in the abyss. The Hairs of His Head are equal in number to the Hidden Worlds; the Forms of His Countenance are the types of the Æons, the Locks of His Beard are the Number of the Exterior Worlds; the Spreading of His Hands is the Manifestation of the Cross: the Extension on the Cross is the Ennead. That which is on the Right, and on the Left, is the Seed of the Cross, it is the Elusive Being. It is the Father; it is the Spring, which sounds in the Silence; it is that which we are ever seeking; it is the Father from whom shineth the Monad like a Spark of Light. It is that which contains all things in the radiance of its splendour. They have received Knowledge, Life, Hope, Peace, Faith, the Second Birth, and the Seal; this is the Ennead which has come forth from the Father, without beginning; He who is his own Father and His Own Mother; the Twelve Abysses which the Pleroma surrounds.

The Twelve Abysses.—The First Abyss is the Universal Spring, from which all Springs come forth.

The Second Abyss is the Universal Wisdom, from which all Wisdoms come forth.

The Third Abyss is the Universal Mystery, from which all Mysteries come forth.

The Fourth Abyss is the Universal Knowledge, from which all Knowledge comes forth.

The Fifth Abyss is the Universal Purity, from which all Purity comes forth.

The Sixth Abyss is that Silence which contains all Silence.

The Seventh Abyss is the Primal Essence, from which all Essence comes forth.

The Eighth Abyss is the Forefather, whence exist all Forefathers.

The Ninth Abyss is the Father of all, and the creator of his own Being, He in Whom is all paternity, Who is himself alone Father of all.

The Tenth Abyss is the All-Powerful One, whence all Powers emanate.

The Eleventh Abyss is the First Invisible One, whence comes all Invisibility.

The Twelfth Abyss is the Truth whence comes all Truth. Truth which is over all things, the Image of the Father, the End of all things, the Mother of all the Æons, that which surroundeth all the Abysses.

Of the Monad and the Demiurgus.—This is the Monad which is unknowable and which no man hath known; that hath no Symbol; all Symbols are in it, it is blessed from generation to generation. This is the Ineffable Father, inconceivable, unthinkable, motionless. This is that to which all things have become similar; they rejoice, they are filled with happiness, they bring forth myriads and myriads of Æons in joy, for they have rejoiced with the Father. These are the worlds in which the STAYROS (Cross) was manifested, and Man came forth from his incorporeal members; this is the Father, the Root of all Being, whose members have emanated from Him. From the Father all names exist, as the Ineffable, Incorruptible, Invisible, Uncompounded, Solitary, Powerful, Omnipotent, there are all Names hidden in the Silence; they are hidden in the Father. This is He whom all the Manifest Worlds see like stars in the Firmament of Night. As men desire to see the Sun, so the Manifest Worlds desire to see the cause of the Mystery which surrounds them. This is He who has ever given life to the Æons; it is by His Word that they exist. The Holy Pleroma exists through His Word. This is the Father, the Second Demiurgos; it is by the Breath of His

Mouth that the Pronoia (that which designs or knows beforehand) conceived the idea of those who have not yet come into existence. They shall exist by His Will for He has ordered that all things shall exist. He created the Holy Pleroma in this way.

Description of the Four Watch Towers of the Universe.—At the Four Watch Towers of the Pleroma are Four Monads, one Monad at each Watch Tower, and Six Defenders at each Gate; in all twenty-four Defenders and twenty-four myriads of Powers at each Gate. Nine enneads at each Gate, ten decads at each Gate, twelve dodecads at each Gate, five pentads of power at each Gate; a Watcher with three faces, one inborn face, one true face, and one ineffable face at each gate; one of these faces looks outward to the face of the Manifest Æons, the other looks in towards the Sētheys (hidden place), the third looks upward; in each monad is the Mntshēre (the power of bringing forth, emanation), there is found aphrēdōn (without heart), with the twelve Christs there is the great Ancestor, also Adam, the Adam of Light, with his three hundred Æons, there is the perfect mind. They border on another abyss of immortality; the ineffable face of the Watcher looking upwards to the Holy of Holies, which is the Infinite, Chief of the Holy Place. This Chief has two faces, one looking towards the Place of the Abyss, and the other towards the abode of the Watcher, who has been named the Server.

The Abyss of Light.—There is an abyss called Light or that which gives Light; in this Abyss is hidden the only Begotten one. He made manifest the Three Powers, He is the Power of Powers. He is Indivisible, and can never separate from himself. All things are open unto him, because with Him is the Power.

Of another Abyss.—There is also another Place which has been called an Abyss, where there are three Paternities. The *First* is the abode of Kalyptō, this is the Hidden God. In the *Second*, there are five trees and in the midst thereof is a Tablet. One Word, The only begotten or *Monogenes*, is on this Tablet, the Twelve Faces of the Mind of all things; and the Prayers of all beings are placed before Him. The Pleroma rejoices because of Him for he has manifested Himself. It is He to whom the Invisible has shown its mystery; it is through Him that Man has come forth. In the *Third*, Paternity is the Silence, and the fountain which the Twelve Christs contemplate, seeing themselves reflected therein. In it also is Agapē (Love) and the Nous (mind) of the Pleroma, and the most holy Pammētōr (mother of all) whence has come the Ennead whose Names are PROTIA, PANTIA, PANGENIA, DOXOPHANIA, DOXOGENIA, DOXOKRATEIA, ARSENOGENIA, LŌIA, IOYĒL. This is the First Unknowable One, the Mother of the Ennead which completes the Decad emanating from the Monad of the Unknowable.

The Incommensurate Abyss.—There is another Vaster Abode in which is hidden a great treasure which surrounds the Pleroma, this is the Incommensurate Abyss, where is a tablet on which are gathered together Three Powers; One Solitary, One Unknowable, and One Infinite. In the midst of which is a Mntshēre (sonship), which is called Christ, the Glorifier; This is He Who glorifies each one and imprints upon Him the Seal of the Father. Who leads all into the Æon of the First Father Who alone Is, He by Whom all exists, and without Whom nothing is.

Abyss of Sētheys, 'the hidden place.—After this is the Abyss of *Sētheys*. This is that, in which are all things surrounding the Twelve Paternities, in the midst of which it dwells. Each Paternity has three Faces. As a Whole they form the number thirty-six. These are they from which the Manifest Ones have received their Seals and Characters, and this is why they have ever received Glory.

There are still Twelve others who surround its Head and who themselves are crowned. They radiate on the worlds which surround them because of the Light of the only begotten which is hidden within Him, and which is sought by all.

Of the Nature of the Only Begotten.—This is He, the True God, the Only Begotten, the All, the Æons of the Pleroma know that it is by Him that they have become Gods, and they have become holy in this Name. This is He of whom John hath said: In the beginning was the Word and the Word was in God, and the Word was God, without whom nothing exists, and what He hath brought forth is Life. This is the Only Begotten Who abode in the monad, who dwelt in it as in a city, and it is the Monad who like a thought is in the Sētheys (hidden place) and the Sētheys is throned in the Temple like a King, and is God. This is the Word of the Demiurgos which commanded the Pleroma to operate; this is the mind of the Demiurgos according to the Law of God the Father; Him that all Creation imploreth as its God and its Lord; unto whom all that is, is in submission.

The Adoration of the Pleroma of the Only Begotten.—The Pleroma (the Perfect Nature) adores Him for His Beauty and His Goodness; those who are in the Pleroma form His Crown; those who are without are under His Feet, and those who are in the midst thereof surround Him. Blessing Him and saying:—" Holy, Holy, Holy, Aaa, Eee, Ēēē, Ooo, Yyy, Ōōō," That is to say, " Thou art the Living, among the Living; thou art Holy, among the Holy Ones; thou *art* among those that are; thou art Father among the Fathers; thou art God among the Gods; thou art Lord among the Lords; thou art Æons among the Æons."

And He blessed them and said:

" Thou art the abode; it is thou who dwellest in the abode."

And He blessed them and said to the Son who is hidden within Him:

" Thou art, Thou art, oh! only begotten, Light and Life and Grace."

Of the Pure Type.—Then Sētheys (hidden one) sent towards the Invisible a Spark; it burned and became a Light for the whole Temple of the Pleroma, and they saw by the Light of the Spark, and they rejoiced, and they sang myriads and myriads of Glorifications in honour of the Sētheys, in honour of the Spark of Light, which had become manifest; seeing that in it was the Image of them all: and they represented the Spark unto themselves as an Illuminated Man of Truth. They named Him PANTOMORPHE (having all forms) and Pure One; they named Him ASALEYTOS (tranquil) and all the Æons called him PANTODYNAMOS (omnipotent). He is the Server of the Æons, and He serves the Pleroma.

And the Indivisible One sent forth the Spark from the Pleroma, and the Three Thunders descended into the Place of the Self-born, and they saw the grace of the Æons, the Light which had been given unto them, and they rejoiced over that which came forth to them. Then were opened the Firmaments, and the Light descended even unto the lowest depths, and towards those who were without form and without likeness. And it was thus that they acquired the likeness of the Light. Some among them rejoiced that the Light had come unto them and that they had become rich. Others wept for they had become poor, and for that which had been taken away. It was thus that the Grace which went forth was received.

This is why it was imprisoned. Glory was given to the Æons which had received the Spark, and Guardians were sent to them who are GAMANĒL, ETREMPSOYKHOS, and AGRAMAS. They bring succour to those who have believed in the Light of the Spark.

Of the Twelve Fountains and the Twelve Paternities.—And in the Abode of the Indivisible are Twelve Fountains, above whom are Twelve Paternities who environ the Indivisible, as do these Abysses or these Firmaments, forming a Crown above the Indivisible, in which is found all species of Life, all the Creatures of the

Three Thunders of the Akhōrētos (established one), of the Infinite, of the Ineffable, of the Silence, of the Unknown, of the Solitary, of the Acaleytos (flux and reflux), of the Prōtōphanēs (first light), of the Self-Born, of the Truth; all these are in Him. In Him are all Creatures, all Knowledge, all Power; in Him all have received the Light, all mind is manifested.

Of the Crown of Three Hundred and Sixty-five Radiations.—This is the Crown that the Father of the Pleroma has placed upon the Indivisible, and it contains three hundred and sixty-five varieties shining and filling the Pleroma with a Perfect and Incorruptible Light. This is the Crown for which all the Immortals cry aloud; and by it and in it they become invisible until the Day of Joy, those who were first manifested by the Will of the Unknowable, that is to say Prōtia, Pantia, Pangenia, and those who are with them. After this, all the Invisible Æons receive from Him their Crown, so that they may go out towards the Invisibles who received their Crown in the Crown of the Invisible, and the Pleroma receives its Perfection from the Incorruptible.

This is why those of them who have taken a body pray, desiring to abandon the body, in order to receive the Crown which is reserved for them in the Incorruptible Æon, and this is the Invisible who was first Æon before that which had rejoiced in the blessings which are above all blessings. The Ennead is composed of twelve Enneads, and in its centre is a place called the Generating Substance of the Gods, this is the Substance of which it is said " He who useth this substance shall be filled with bread and his borders shall be enlarged." And also: " The Master of the field which has been cultivated possesses all good." And all these powers which are in the substance which engenders the gods have received the Crown. It is because of the Crown which is upon their head that they know if the Paralēmptor (creative force) have gone forth from the Indivisible or not.

Of the Universal Mother.—From them is the Universal

Mother in whom are seven Wisdoms, Nine Enneads, Ten Decads, and in the midst of whom is a great Kanoyn (Centre of equilibrium); a great Invisible One stands above with a Great Inborn One, a great Akhōrētos (Established one), which have three faces; and Prayer, Benediction and the Hymn of the Creatures are placed upon this Kanoyn which is in the midst of the Universal Mother, and the Wisdoms and the Enneads and the Decads. And these stood upright upon the Kanoyn made perfect by the fruit of the Æons, those who have decreed that the Hidden only begotten in the Indivisible should be with them, and the Powers around Him say :

Hymn of the Powers surrounding the Only Begotten One. —" It is through Thee that we are glorified and by thee we see the Father of the Pleroma Aaaōōō and the Mother of all blessings ; She is hidden within all things and is the thought of all the Æons, the Ennoia (Conception or idea) of all the Gods and all the Lords ; She is the knowledge of all the Invisible Ones and her Reflection is the Mother of all the Akhōrētos (Established ones), the Power of the Infinite. It is because of Thy Reflection, Oh, only begotten that we see thee, that we hasten to thee, that we hold to thee, that we receive the Incorruptible Crown ; that which is known by itself. Glory unto Thee, Oh, only begotten for ever." And all of them said " Amen " together ; and they became a body luminous, which traversed the Æons of the Indivisible until they came to the only begotten who is in the Monad, the Abode of tranquillity and Solitude, and they received grace from the only begotten, that is to say from his Christhood, and the Crown Eternal. This is the Father of all the Sparks of Light, the Chief of all Immortal Bodies, that which is the Cause of the Resurrection of the Body.

The Incommensurate Abyss and the Five Powers, Love, Hope, Faith, Knowledge and Peace.—And in the midst of the Incommensurate Abyss are Five Powers called by these Ineffable Names:—The first is AGAPE (Love), and from it proceeds all love; the second is ELPIS (Hope), and through it we hope in the Only-Begotten Son of God; the third is PISTIS (Faith), it is through it we believe the mysteries of the Ineffable; the fourth is GNOSIS (Knowledge); through her we know the First Father through Whom we exist, the Mystery of Silence which speaks before all things; which is hidden; the First Monad, through which the Pleroma became Substance; upon the head of this mystery the Three hundred and Sixty-Five Substances form a Crown like the Hair of Man, and the Temple of the Pleroma is like the ground under His Feet; this is the gate of God. The fifth is EIRĒNE (Peace), and through it Peace is given to all, those who are without and those who are within, because it is in her all things are created, the Incommensurable Abyss, that in which subsist Three hundred and Sixty-Five Paternities through whom we obtain the divisions of the Year.

The Whole Pleroma was troubled, the Abyss and all that was therein was moved, they hastened away toward the Æon of the Mother. The Mystery gave commandment that the veils of the Æons should be withdrawn until the Watcher had once more established them, and the Watcher established the Æons once more as it is written :

" He has established the Earth and she shall not be moved."

Also :

" The Earth is dissolved, and all that was upon her."

Then the Triple Power went forth, the Son was hidden within Him and the Crown of Confirmation was upon His Head, making myriads and myriads of Glories and they cried :

" Make straight the way of the Lord and Receive the Grace of God : all your Æons shall be filled with the Grace of the Only Begotten Son and the Holy Father, and perfected it shall stand above the Incommensurable

Abyss. In Him is found all perfection and from His plenitude we have received Grace."

The Establishment of the Incommensurate Abyss.—Then the Æon was confirmed and no longer trembled: and the Father confirmed it that it feared no more, and the Æon of the Mother was filled with those who until then had been hidden within the First Father, from whom came the mystery, in order that His Son might re-establish the Pleroma in knowledge which should enclose the Pleroma.

The Emanation of the Word.—Then Sētheys (hidden place) sent forth a Demiurgos Word having with it a cloud of Powers with crowns upon their heads, throwing out rays, and the brilliance of their bodies made them manifest. The Word which went forth from their Mouths was Eternal Life, and the Light which went from their Eyes was its resting-place; the movement of their hands showed the Path towards the Place whence they came; the Extension of their hands gives stability; the hearing of their ears is the perception which is in their Hearts; their union is the re-union of Israel; their comprehension of themselves is the contemplation of the Word; the number of their fingers is the number of which it is written:—

" Those who count the multitude of the Stars, and who give them each their name."

And the union of the Demiurgos Word was with those who came forth from the trembling which had been, and they became one and the same thing as it is written:—

" They have become one and the same in the only One."

Then the Demiurgos Word became a powerful God, Lord, Saviour, Christ, King, Good, Father, Mother. It is He of whom the Work was Good. He was glorified, and became Father for those who believed in him; he became Law in the Aphrōdonia and Powerful.

The Great Mother and her order.—The All-Established-

One went forth; she had a crown upon her head and she placed it upon those who believed. And the Virgin-Mother, the Power of the Æons, the Hierarchy of its Worlds was according to the order of the Interior Place. She established in herself the Brilliance of the Light after the Type of the Monad; she established the Katalyptos (judgments) which surrounded her; she established the Propatōr (Great Ancestor) according to the Type of the Indivisible and the twelve Christs which surrounded them; having crowns on their heads and a seal of glory in their right hands; Love was in the midst of them, a Face of the Triple Force in the Fountain and a Kanoyn (place of rest) which the Twelve Paternities surrounded, in which was hidden a mntshēre (procreative force). She established the Self-Father according to the Type of the Ennead without a symbol, she gave him power over the Father who begot him, she crowned him with all Glory, she gave him Love, Peace, Truth, and myriads of Powers, in order that he might gather together those who had been dispersed by the trembling which had taken place at the moment when he came forth with joy.

As to the Lord of the Pleroma Who had the Power of Life and Death, she established the First-begotten son, after the Type of the Triple Force, she gave Him Nine times an Ennead; she gave Him ten times five Decads, in order that he should have the Force to fight out the combat imposed upon him, and she gave him the first-fruits of the mntshēre (creative force) which was in her. He had the power to become the Triple Force, and He received the promise of mntshēre, promise which was given to the Pleroma for His sake; He accepted the combat which was entrusted to Him, and he made all that was pure in matter to rise; he made a world, an Æon, a City; this is the World that is called Incorruptibility and Jerusalem. It is also called the New Earth and Autotelēs (complete in itself); and also without King. This Earth is the Earth which brings forth the

Gods; an Earth-nourishing Life; this is she that the Great Mother commanded to be established; this is why the Mother placed the orders of the hierarchies in this Earth, she has established there the Pronoia (Foresight) and Love. This is the Earth of which it is written:—
"Earth which drinks rain a multitude of times."

That is to say which multiplies the Light in her thousands and thousands of times from her going forth to her return, that is to say that for which man is called sensible. It is formed and created according to the type of this earth: and this it is that the Protogenitor (First-begetter) has himself saved from dispersion.

Because of this the Father of all those in the Pleroma has sent a crown on which is set forth the names of all those in the Pleroma.

Of the Crown.—This is the Crown of which it is written:—

"It was given to Solomon on the day of the Exaltation of his heart."

The First Monad sent him an ineffable garment which was all Light, all Life, all Love, all Hope, all Faith, all Wisdom, all Understanding, all Truth, all Peace, all Evidence, all Universal Mother, all-universal mystery, all Universal Fountain, all universal perfection . . . The whole Pleroma is in it, and it is that in which the Pleroma is manifested, and all things are known to her. She gave all Light from her ineffable Light . . . she gave them a veil which envelopes them on all sides . . . she divided them according to hierarchies. Then that which WAS separated from that which WAS NOT, and that which WAS NOT was the evil which manifested as matter, and the Garment of Power separated that which existed from that which did not exist.

The Order of the really existing ones.—She called that which existed AIŌNIOS, and that which did not exist HYLĒ. She gave a law to those who exist, and she made the Mother the ruler. She gave Ten Æons, each with a myriad of Powers, a monad and an Ennead in each Æon. She placed in her a ray from the Universal Mother, and she gave her the Power to be invisible, that no man might see her. She established within her a great Kanoyn (place of equilibrium) over which were three powers, an Unbegotten, Asaleytos (tranquillity) and Purity. She gave her twelve other Powers crowned and surrounding her. And Seven Stratelates (Leaders of armies), which have the seal of the all-perfect, and they have upon their heads a crown of twelve diamonds which come from Adam, the Man of Diamond.

The Establishment of the First Father.—She established the Protopatōr (First Father) in her Æons; she gave him the Power of the Paternity and of obedience; she gave him a crown of twelve kinds, and a Power of triple force, which is Pantodynamos (First power), and she gave him the mntshēre (power of emanation), and thousands of glories and the power of Life and Death. The Power which was given to the Propatōr was called PROTŌPHANĒS (First light) because it was that which was first manifested; it was called unbegotten, because no one had created it; it was called also ineffable and nameless. Also Autogenēs (self-generated) and also Autoteletos (complete in itself) because it manifested by its own will. Also Autodoxastos (self-effulgent), because it manifested itself with the glories which were within it; also Invisible because it was hidden. She gave it also another Power, that of making Light appear, that which one calls Holy; it is the Protia, that is, the first; it is called Pantia, that is, that in which all things are; also Pangenia, that which has brought forth all things; also Doxogenia, that which has brought forth glory; also Doxophania, that which has manifested glory, also Doxokrateia, because it rules glory, also Arsenogenia, because she brings forth sons, also Loia, meaning God with us, also Ioyel, meaning God Eternal, who has commanded that the Powers should appear, also Paneia, of which the meaning is Manifestation. The angel which appears with them is that of the glories named Doxogenes and Doxophanes, of which the interpretation is that which begets glory and which manifests glory, because it is one of these glories which stand round the great power named Doxokratōr, because in its manifestation it has dominion over the great glories. Such are the powers which were given to the Propatōr placed in the Æon of the mother, to him were given myriads of glories, angels, Archangels, liturgies, to the end that he should serve material things. He was given power over all things. He made a great Æon, and placed within it a great Pleroma, a great Temple, and all the Powers that he had taken, that he had placed in Himself, and He rejoiced with them and He brought forth his creations once more according to the order of the Father given in silence, who had sent these riches to him, and the crown of the Paternity was given to him because he had made it Father of that which existed after Him.

Then he cried saying:

" My children that I bring forth anew in order that Christ should be formed in you."

Also :

" I am ready to stand up with a Holy Virgin before Christ the Bridegroom."

But when He had seen the grace which the Hidden Father had given to Him, he wished to turn the Pleroma towards the Father Whose Will it was that the Pleroma should turn towards Him.

And when the Mother saw all the splendours which were given to her propator, she rejoiced greatly, she exulted, that is why she said :

" My Heart is rejoiced and My Voice is exalted."

The rejoicing of the Great Mother.—Then she cried towards the Infinite Power which stood near the Æon of the Father, this great Power of Glory, this which among the glories is called Thrice Begotten. This is also called Trigenēs also Harmēs. She also took that which is hidden in all places, in order that it might send her the Mother of that which is withdrawn ; the Hidden Father sent the mystery which is round about all the Æons and the Glories which formed the Crown of the Panteles, that is to say, of the Perfect One, so that it should put it upon the head of the Hidden Indivisible, Incorruptible and Unbegotten, with the Great Powers of their Company called Arsenogenia, which fill all the Æons of Glory. Thus did the Pleroma receive from Him the Crown.

The Bringer into being of himself is established.—Then she established Auto-Pator Father and Eternal; she gave to him the Æon of the Hidden in which all things are in the form of Kinds, Figures, Images, Forms, Interrogations, Differences and Variations, that which counts and that which is counted, that which thinks and that which is thought. She made of it a garment covering all that was contained therein so that it might give to him that asks. She gave it Ten Powers, Nine Enneads, Five Æons, and Phōstēr (Lights) and gave Him Power over all Hidden Things, so that He might give Grace to those who had fought, who had left behind them matter, and who had hastened towards the Æon of Autopator; they had claimed the promise which had been spoken:—

"Those who abandon Father, Mother, Brother, Sister, Wife, Children, Riches, who take up their Cross and follow Me, they shall receive the promises that I have promised to them, and I will give them the mystery of the Hidden Father because they have fulfilled the purpose of their being and have flown before that which pursued them with injustice."

He gave them Glory, Joy, Exaltation, Happiness, Peace, Hope, Faith, Love, and Truth which cannot change. This is the Ennead with which he rewards those who fly from matter. They become happy, they become perfect, they know God and Truth, they understand the mystery which has operated in mankind, why he was manifested, in order that they might live they were made blind, and because of Him the Word was manifested that he might know it, that they who take up the Cross should become God and should become perfect.

The First Begotten is established.—Then the Mother established the Prōtōgennētōr as Her Son. She gave Him Power, she gave him armies of angels and archangels and Twelve Powers; she gave him a garment in which all bodies should exist, bodies of Fire, Water, Air, Earth, Wind, Angels, Archangels, Powers, Forces, Gods, Lords, in a word all bodies so that nothing should prevent him from rising to the heights or descending to the depths of the Noun. This is the Prōtogenitōr (First Begetter), that which is without and that which is within hath promised all things which please Him and He discerns what is in all matter and He broodeth over Her like a bird spreading its Wings over its Eggs. It is thus that the Prōtōgennētōr acted towards matter and He made myriads and myriads of Ideas to ascend. When matter was warm, it produced a multitude of Powers, it grew like a plant, and divided them according to Type and Idea; so it gave them a Law of Life to glorify God, to bless Him, to seek Whom He was and what he was, so that they might behold with wonder the place from whence they came, seeing how narrow and sad it was and that they could not return but that they should go to that which had given them a law, and which had caused them to come forth from the shadows of matter, which was their Mother. He said to them:

" Let there be Light."

For they did not know whether Light existed or not. Then he gave them commandment that they should not destroy themselves, and He left them to go towards the abode of the Mother of the Pleroma, to the Prōpatōr, and the Self-Father, in order that they should surpass those who had gone forth from matter. And the Mother of the Pleroma, the Prōpatōr, and the Self-Father, and the Prōgennētōr, and the Powers of the Æon of the Mother raised up a great Hymn blessing the One Alone, and saying to him:

These all having been established raise a Hymn of Praise.
—" Thou art the Only Infinite, Thou art the only Abyss, Thou art the only Unknown, it is Thee that all have sought and have not found, for no man may know Thee against Thy Will and no man may bless Thee against thy Will, Thy Will alone. It is Thy Will alone which is an Abode for thee, for nothing can be an Abode for thee since thou art the abode of all things. I invoke thee that thou shouldst give a hierarchy to those of the world and that thou shouldst dispose the seeds thereof according to Thy Will ; let us not be saddened, for nothing has yet been made sad by thee. No man knoweth Thy Design. All those that are without and those that are within have need of Thee, for Thou art the only Akhōrētos (Established one), Thou art the only Indivisible, Thou art the Only Anousios (One without mind), Thou art the only one who hath given a Symbol to thy creatures, and who hath made them manifest from Thyself, Thou art the Demiurgos of that which is not yet manifested, for these things that Thou knowest alone and that we know not, can only be shown to us by thee when we invoke Thee because of them, in order that thou mayest make them plain to our comprehension, for Thou alone canst do so. Thou alone hast risen unto the Hidden Worlds, so that they may know thee, thou hast made them able to know thee for Thou hast given them birth from thy incorporeal body, and thou hast produced man from the emanation of thy mind, in a Dianoia (Discursive thought) and a perfect thought ; It is a man, produced by the mind, to whom thought gave form. It is Thou Who hast given all blessings to man, and he wears them as a garment ; they are both a covering and a safeguard. It is man that the Pleroma has desired to know. Thou alone hast ordered that Man should be manifested in order that thou shouldst be known through him. Thou hast produced him and hast appeared according to Thy Will. Thee I invoke Oh ! Father of all Paternity, Lord of all Lords, I entreat

thee to give hierarchy to my ideas and to my seed, that I may rejoice in Thy Name and thy virtue, oh! Only Monarch, Only Immutable One. Give me virtue that I may make known unto my offspring that thou art their Saviour."

And when the Mother had finished praying unto the Infinite, the Unknowable, that which filled the Pleroma and which gave them eternal life, he heard her and those who are with her, those which belong to her and he sent to them a power from Mankind, that which their hearts desired.

The Manifestation.—And the Infinite sent forth the Infinite Spark, all the Æons praised it in the places where they were hidden before they were manifested from without the Infinite Father, whence also the Pleroma was manifested, and that which was hidden within it. The Powers of the hidden Æons followed her until they were manifested and they became the Temple of the Pleroma. She hid herself among the Powers who had gone forth from the Hidden Place, she made of them a World and she placed it within the Temple. Then the Powers of the Pleroma saw her and they loved her. She blessed them with ineffable hymns not to be spoken by the Tongue of Man; hymns worthy to be meditated in the inmost heart. She received their hymn and she made of it a veil surrounding their worlds like a wall, and she departed towards the limits of the Mother of the Pleroma, and she stood above the Universal Æon. The Pleroma was moved in the presence of the Lord of the Universe, the Æon was troubled and breathed not, for it had seen what it could not understand.

The Lord of Glory was Enthroned.—The Lord of glory was enthroned; and he parted matter into two parts and into two places, and he fixed the limits of each, and he instructed them that they had proceeded from the only Father and the Only Mother; to those who hastened to him and adored him he gave a place on the right and he gave them the gift of Life Eternal and Immortality. He named the place on the right side of Him, the Earth of Life, and the place on the Left Side of Him the Earth of Death, and that on the right the Earth of Light, that on the Left the Earth of Shadows; that on the right the earth of repose, that on the left the earth of sorrow; he placed limits between them and veils that they should not behold one another; and he gave numberless glories to those who had adored him, and he made them Lords over those who had resisted and were opposed to him. He disposed the earth on his right hand unto numerous habitations, and he placed it in each hierarchy, each Æon, each World, each Heaven, each firmament, in the Heavens, in every place, in every Khōrēma. He gave them laws, he gave them commandment, saying:

"Keep my words and I will give you Life Eternal, I will send you powers, I will establish powerful spirits within you, and I will give you such power as you desire; none shall be able to prevent you doing that which you will; you shall produce Æons, Worlds and Heavens, to the end that the Spirits of the Intellectual Spheres may come and abide with you; you shall become Gods; you shall know that you have come forth from God; and you shall see God in yourselves; He will dwell in your Æon."

These Words the Lord of the Pleroma having spoken, he retired from them and hid himself away. And those who were produced from matter rejoiced that their thought had been accomplished; and they made glad because they had gone forth from the narrow and sad place; and they prayed the Hidden Mystery, saying:

Prayer of those who were produced from matter.—" Give unto us the Power to create for ourselves Æons, and the Worlds that thou hast spoken of, Lord, as thou hast sworn unto thy servants, for thou alone art immovable, thou art the only Infinite, the only Akhōrētos (established one), thou art the only unbegotten, born from thyself,

self-generated, thou art the Akaleytos, and the Unknowable, thou art the Silence, the Love, and the Fountain of the Pleroma; thou alone art the Immaterial; thou alone hast no soil nor stain; Ineffable in thy generation; Inconceivable in thy manifestation. Hear me, then, Oh Incorruptible Father, Immortal Father, God of the Hidden Being, only Light and Life, only Invisible, only Indivisible, only Amiantos (undefiled), only Alampetos (concealed one), Primal Being. Nothing was before thou wast. Listen to this prayer, which we offer to those which are hidden. Hear us; send us Incorporeal Spirits that they may dwell with us, and teach us what thou hast promised; that they may dwell in us, and that we may become their habitation, for it is thy will that it should be so; so let it be. Dispose our work and establish it according to thy will, and according to the disposition of the hidden Æons dispose of us as thou wilt; for we are thine."

Answer to the Prayer.—And he heard their voice, and he sent them powers capable of discernment, knowing the disposition of the Hidden Æons; he sent them according to the disposition of that which is hidden; he established the hierarchy according to the hierarchies of that which is above, and according to the secret disposition. They began from the lowest even unto the highest, in order that the instructions should unite them to their companions. He created the aërial regions as a place of habitation for those who had gone forth, where they might dwell until those who were beneath them had become established; then he created the Abode of Truth; within the Centre of this, the Abode of Repentance; within that, the Antitype of Aerodios (air gods); within that, the Antitype of the Auto-genēs (Self-born); in this place Purification was performed in the name of Auto-genēs, which is God over them; and Powers are placed here upon the Source of the Waters of Life. These are the names of power which are set over the Waters of Life, Michar and Micheu, and they are purified in the name of Barpharangos. Within these are the Æons of Wisdom, and again Absolute Truth, and the Pistis Sofia abides there, also the Proontos, Jesus, Lord of Life, Aerodios, and his Twelve Æons. There are placed Cellaō, Eleinos, Zōgenethlēs, Selmelhke, and the Auto-genēs of the Æons.

The Book of the Grand Words of each Mystery.

Jesus said unto His disciples gathered round about Him: to the Twelve, and the Holy Women that were with them:—

Of the Æon of Treasure.—"Gather round me, O my Disciples, men and women, so that I may tell you the mysteries of the Æon of Treasure hidden in the Invisible God, which no man knoweth; and if you perform them the Æons of the Invisible God will not be able to rise up against you, for they are great mysteries of the Holy of Holies. If you perform them the Arkhons (Rulers) of the Æons cannot resist them nor torture you; but the Paralēmptēs (Creative force) of the Æon of Treasure can draw the soul from the body, so that it can traverse all the Æons and the abode of the Invisible God, and lead it unto the Æon of Treasure. And all conscious or unconscious sin shall be wiped out; a pure light shall be evolved; and the soul passing from world to world shall rest in it until it arrives at the Æon of Treasure. Then it shall pass into the Sanctuary of the Guardians of the Æon of Treasure; beyond this to the Sanctuary of the three Amen; beyond this to the Sanctuary of Gemini; beyond this to the Sanctuary of the Three Thunders; beyond this to the Sanctuary of the Five Trees; beyond this to the Sanctuary of the Seven Voices; beyond this into the Abode which is in the Sanctuary. This is the Abode of Akhōrētos (Established one) of the Æon of Treasure. And all these hierarchies will give you their Seals and their Mysteries, because your soul shall have received the mystery before being drawn forth from the body."

When he had finished these words he spake, and said to them:

Of Keeping Secret the Mysteries.—"The Mysteries which I give unto you, treasure them in your hearts, and give them unto no man who is unworthy; neither to Father, nor Mother, nor brother, nor sister, nor unto thy kindred, neither for food, nor for drink, nor for lust, nor for gold, nor for silver, nor for any of the goods of this World; treasure them, give them unto no man for gold, give them unto no unholy woman, nor to any man who believes in the eighty-two * rulers, or to those who serve them. Reveal them not unto those who serve the eighth power of the great Arkhon. Those are they who delight in foulness. We know the Truth and we worship the Truth. But the God of these is an evil God. Listen unto me and I will instruct you as to the disposition of this God. He is the Third Power of the Great Arkhon. His name is Tarikhthas, Son of Sabaōth Adamas: he is the enemy of the Kingdom of Heaven; his face is featureless, his teeth stand out from his mouth, and behind him is the face of a lion. Beware, and give not our mysteries unto those who believe in him; tell them not unto such men, neither the Abode of the Treasure nor those who dwell therein, for it is this Æon which the Immutable God hath formulated.

"Tell not, except to those who are worthy, the mysteries of the Æon of Treasure; they are beyond the World; beyond all things, and their Gods, and their Divinities; let not the mysteries be profaned, for those who belong to them are the children of Light, hearing one another, obeying one another, children of the Æon of Treasure.

"Behold what I tell you on the subject of these mysteries. Now, therefore, since you have left your fathers, your mothers, your brothers, and the whole

---

* This may be read twelve.

world, to follow me, since you have accomplished all the Commandments that I have given unto you; listen unto the mysteries.

"Verily, verily, I say unto you, I will give you the mysteries of the Twelve Divine Æons, and of their Paralēmptor (creative force), and the manner of invoking them so as to enter into their abodes. I will also give unto you the mysteries of the Divine Invisibility, and of their Paralēmptor. After that I will teach you the mystery of those in the midst, and their Paralēmptor. Then I will give you the mystery of those upon the Right Hand, and their Paralēmptor.

Of the Three Baptisms.—"But before this I must give you the Three Baptisms; the Baptism of Water, the Baptism of Fire, the Baptism of the Holy Spirit, and I will give unto you the mystery of exorcising the evil influences of the Arkhons; and after that I will give you the Sanctifying Grace of the Breath of Life (Ruach Elohim). And before all things, command those on whom you bestow these mysteries not to swear falsely, nor to swear at all, neither to commit fornication, nor adultery, nor theft, nor to covet silver or gold, nor to take in vain the Names of the Arkhons, nor of their Angels; let them not be fraudulent, nor evil speaking, nor lying, nor slandering; but let their yes mean yes, and their no, no; in a word, let them observe the Holy Commandments."

The disciples humble themselves.—And it came to pass that when Jesus had finished saying these things unto his disciples they were filled with a great sorrow; and they threw themselves at His Feet weeping and crying out. They said unto Him:

"Lord, why hast thou said unto us, I will give thee the mystery of Treasure?"

But His Heart was troubled because of His Disciples, for they had abandoned all things and had followed him for twelve years, keeping the commandments which he had given them; and he replied unto them, saying:

Of the Forgiveness of Sins.—"Verily I say unto you, I will make known unto you the Mysteries of the Treasure and the Guardians of the Three Gates of the Æon of Treasure and all the mysteries which I have mentioned unto you. Verily, I will give them unto you, I command you to perform the mystery of the Five Trees, the Mystery of the Seven Voices, and the Mystery of the Great Name, which is the Supreme Treasure surrounding the Æon of Treasure; for he who performs these, needs no other mystery of the kingdom of Light unless it be the Mystery of the Remission of Sins. It is necessary that He who believes in the Kingdom of Treasure should perform the mystery of the Remission of Sins that he may be purified, and the sins that he has committed be wiped out so that he may become a pure light and may enter into the Treasure of Treasures. And I say unto you while they are yet upon earth they shall inherit the Kingdom of God, for their part is in the Æon of Treasure; they are Immortal Gods; and when those who have received the mystery of the Remission of Sins go forth from their bodies all the Æons fly before them, they hide themselves in the West, in the region which is on the left, because of the Glory of the Soul who has received the mystery of the Remission of Sins. And their souls shall come unto the gate of the Æon of Treasure, and the Guardian of the Gates shall open unto them.

Of the other Mysteries.—"When they have arrived at the Hierarchies of Treasure other hierarchies shall seal them with their seals, shall give unto them the Grand Name of their Mysteries, and shall make them enter into their Sanctuaries. Thus shall they pass through the hierarchies of the Five Trees, the Seven Voices, the Apatōr, the Tripneymatos, the Ieoy, Sigē, or the Silence. I will also give you all Mysteries, and you shall be made perfect in the mysteries of the Kingdom of Treasure, and you shall be called Sons of the Pleroma, perfect in all mysteries."

And it came to pass that Jesus said unto his Disciples:—

"Come unto me and receive the Three Baptisms before I tell you the Mystery of the Arkhons."

And the men and women gathered together around him. Jesus said unto them:

"Go unto Galilee; find a man or a woman whose iniquity is pardoned, that is to say one who has begun to live a pure life. Take two vessels of wine from the hands of such an one, and bring me branches of a vine."

The Baptism of Water.—The disciples brought the wine, and the branches of vine. Then Jesus disposed an offering for sacrifice; he placed a cup of wine to the left and to the right of the offering, he placed juniper berries upon the offering with dried cinnamon, and spikenard; he made his disciples clothe themselves in garments of linen, and put in their mouths roots of the herb cynocephalus. He placed in their two hands the number of the Seven Voices which is 9,879, he also placed in their hands the Solar herb. He placed His disciples before the offering, and Jesus stood on the other side of it. He spread a linen cloth, and placed upon it a cup of wine, and pieces of bread equal in number to his disciples, He put branches of olive upon the place of the offering, and He crowned them with wreaths of olive. Jesus marked His disciple with this Seal:

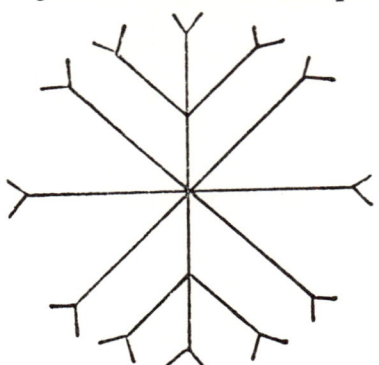

of which the interpretation is Eēzōzaz, and the Name Sazapharas. Jesus with His disciples went to the Four Quarters. He gave them commandment each to place their feet by the side of his neighbours'. He prayed and said:

"Iōazazeth Azazē Asazēth, Amēn, Amēn, Amēn: Eiazei Eaizei Khēth Zaēth Zaēth Amēn, Amēn, Amēn, Abrazazaza Baozazzaz Zazzoos Amēn, Amēn, Amēn; Azaakhazarakha Zarakha Zareatho Zarbathōz Zaraei Zaraei Zaraei Azarakha Kharza Barkha Thazath Thazath, Thazath, Amēn, Amēn, Amēn. Hear me, oh my Father, Father of all paternity, the infinite who abides in the Æon of Treasure whence come the five parastates serving the seven Virgins of Treasure, propitious to the Baptism of Life, and of whom the ineffable names are—Astrapa, Tephoiode, Ontonios, Sinētos, Lakhon, Politanos, Opakis, Paidros, Odontokhoos, Diaktios, Knēsion, Dromos, Eyidenos, Polypaidos, Entropon, may they come to baptize my disciples with the waters of Life from the Seven Virgins of Treasure, may they grant them remission of sins, purify their iniquities, and write their names in the Book of the Kingdom of Life. And if thou hearest me, if thou takest pity on my disciples, if thou inscribest their names in the Book of the Inheritance of the Kingdom of Light, if thou wilt remit their sins, if thou wilt wash out their iniquities, grant us our prayer and permit the Zorokothora to bring the water of the baptism of Life, and place it in one of these cups of wine."

And in a moment the miracle which Jesus had desired took place: the wine which was on the right of the sacrifice was changed into water. The disciples came before Jesus who baptized them, gave them of the sacrifice and sealed them with this Seal:

The Disciples rejoiced with a great joy because their sins had been remitted, their iniquities covered, and their names inscribed as heirs of the Kingdom of Light; for they had been baptised in the Waters of Life from the Seven Virgins of Treasure, and they had received the sacred and holy seal. And it came to pass that Jesus continued to speak and said unto his disciples :—

The Baptism of Fire.—" Bring me branches of vine, that you may receive the baptism of fire."

And the disciples brought him branches of vine which he placed upon the incense : he put myrrh upon it, he added incense of Lebanon, lentisk of mastic, Spikenard, Juniper flowers, turpentine and gum. He spread on the place of the offering a linen cloth, and placed thereon a cup of wine, and pieces of bread equal in number to his disciples, and they were again clothed in linen garments and crowned with the herb called vervain of Osiris, and He put in their mouths the herb called cynocephalus, and in their two hands the number of the Seven Voices which was 9,879. He also gave into their hands the herb marigold. He put bunches of the same flowers beneath their feet and placed before them the aromatic incense which he had prepared. He gave them commandment to place their feet each by the side of his neighbours'. And He stood on the other side of the Incense and sealed them with this seal :

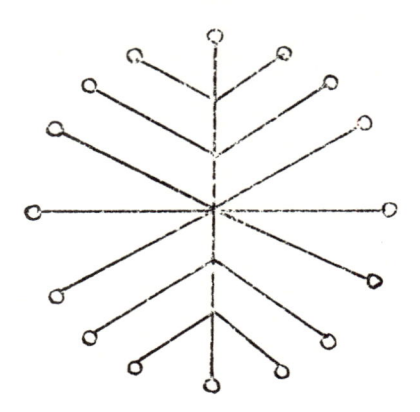

of which the name is THĒZAĒEZ and the interpretation ZŌZAĒZ. Jesus turned himself to the Four Quarters with his Disciples and prayed saying :—

" Hear me, oh my Father, Father of all Paternity, Infinite Light, render these my disciples worthy to receive the Baptism of Fire, forgive their sins, purify the iniquities which they have committed consciously or unconsciously, those which they have committed from their childhood even unto this day, their thoughtless words, their evil speech, their false witness, their thefts, their lies, their deceitful calumnies, their fornications, their adulteries, their covetousness, their avarice, and all the sins that they may have committed, efface them, purify them from them, and let the ZOROKOTHORA come in secret and bring them the Water of the Baptism of Fire of the Virgin of Treasure: Hear me, oh my Father; I invoke thy Incorruptible Names hidden in the Æons for ever. AZARAKAZA AAMATHKRATITATH IŌIŌIŌ ZAMĒN ZAMĒN ZAMĒN IAŌTH IAŌTH IAŌTH PHAŌPH PHAŌPH PHAŌPH KHIŌEPHOZPE KHENOBINYTH ZARLAI LAZARLAI LAIZAI, AMĒN AMĒN ; ZAZIZAYAH NEBEOYNISPH PHAMOY PHAMOY PHAMOY AMOYNAI AMOYNAI AMOYNAI AMĒN ΛMĒN AMĒN ZAZAZAZI ETAZAZA ZŌTHAZAZAZA. Hear me, my Father, Father of all paternities, Infinite Light, I invoke thy Incorruptible Name which is in the Æon of Light that ZOROKOTHORA should send the Water of the Fiery Baptism from the Virgin of Light to the end that I may baptise my disciples. Hear me again, oh my Father, Father of all Paternity, Infinite Light, that the Virgin of Light may come, that she may baptise my disciples with Fire, that she may pardon their sins, purify their iniquities, for I invoke thy Incorruptible Name which is ZOTHŌOZA THOITHAZAZZAŌTH AMĒN AMĒN AMĒN. Hear me also, Oh Virgin of Light, oh Judge of Truth, forgive the sins of my disciples; and if, oh my Father, thou blottest out their iniquities, may they be written down heirs of the Kingdom of Light, and to this end perform a miracle upon these censers of sweet smelling perfume."

And in a moment the miracle occurred. And Jesus baptised His disciples and gave them sacrifice, and he sealed their foreheads with the seal of the Virgin of Light. And the disciples rejoiced that they had received the baptism of Fire, and the Seal for the remission of sins, and their names were inscribed as heirs of the Kingdom of Light. Behold the Seal:

And it came to pass that Jesus said unto his Disciples: "Now you, having received the baptism of water and the baptism of Fire, come unto me that you may receive the baptism of the Holy Spirit."

Baptism of the Holy Spirit.—He placed the perfumes of the baptism of the Spirit in their places, and over them branches of olive, of juniper, and cinnamon, of dried saffron, mastic gum, cinnamum, myrrh, and balm with honey. He put two cups of wine to the right and left of the perfume, besides loaves of bread, equal in number to his disciples. Jesus marked his disciples with this seal:

the name of which is ZAKZŌZA and the interpretation THŌZŌNŌZ. And it came to pass when they were marked with the seal, Jesus standing behind the perfumes, disposed his disciples in front of them; they were clothed in garments of linen; the number of the mystery of the seven Voices was in their two hands, it is 9,879. Jesus spake and said, "Hear me, oh my Father, Father of all Paternity, Infinite Light, I invoke thee by the Incorruptible names of the Æon of Light ZAZAZAOY, ZŌTHZAZŌTH, THOZAXAZŌTH, KENOYBINYE, ATHAĖĖY, ŌZĖŌZAEOZ, KROMBLATH. Hear me, oh my Father, Father of all Paternities, Infinite Light, for I invoke the Incorruptible names of the Æon of Light. Take away the sins of my disciples, cleanse them from the iniquities which they have committed knowingly or unknowingly, the evil which they have committed from their infancy even unto this day; write their names in the Book of the Inheritance of the Kingdom of Light. If Thou takest away their sins, if Thou purifiest their iniquities, if Thou writest their names in the book of the inheritance of the Kingdom of Light, grant, oh my Father, a miracle."

And even as he spoke the miracle took place upon the offering. And he baptised all his disciples with the baptism of the Holy Spirit. They partook of the offering, and he marked their foreheads with the seal of the Seven Virgins of Light to the end that their names should be written in the inheritance of the Kingdom of Light. And the Disciples rejoiced with a great joy, that they had received the baptism of the Holy Spirit and the Seal which took away sin and purified iniquity, for their names had been written in the Inheritance of the Kingdom of Light.

Behold the seal:

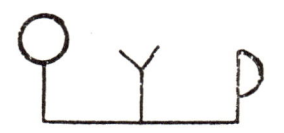

And when Jesus had performed this mystery, all his
disciples stood clothed in garments of linen, crowned
with morsyne, a branch of the Cretan Cynocephalus
upon their mouths, and mugwort in their two hands.
Their feet were placed one against the other, and they
turned towards the four quarters of the World.

And it came about that Jesus disposed the perfumes
in the manner necessary for the performance of the
mystery of the deliverance of his disciples from the evil
desires of the Arkhons. He placed a censer upon the
androsace. He took branches of vine, juniper, cinna-
mon-leaves, and sweet flag, also loadstone, agate stone,
and incense. He clothed his disciples in garments of
linen, he crowned them with mugwort, and placed
incense in their mouths; he put the number of the First
Amen into one of their hands, and he placed their feet side
by side standing before the perfumes. Jesus marked his
disciples with this seal:

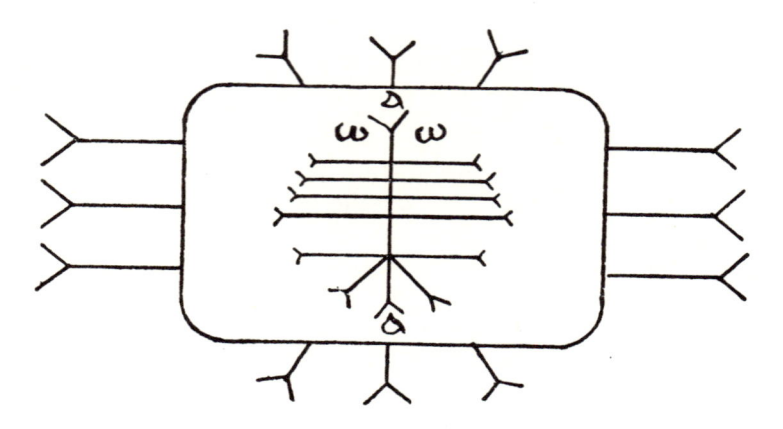

of which the true name is ZĒZĒŌIAZŌZ and the interpretation is ZŌZŌZAI. When Jesus had marked his disciples
with this seal, he took his place on the other side of the
perfumes and he prayed, saying:—" Hear me, oh my
Father, Father of all Paternities, Infinite Light, for I

invoke thee in the incorruptible names of the Æon of Light NĒRĒTĒR, ZOPHONĒR, ZOILTHOZOYBAO, XOYBAŌ, AMĒN, AMĒN, AMĒN. Hear me, oh! my Father, may the Sabaōth Adamos and all the Arkhons come forth and take away the iniquities of my disciples." When he had uttered these words, having turned unto the four quarters of the World with his disciples, he imprinted upon them the mark of the Second Amen which is this:

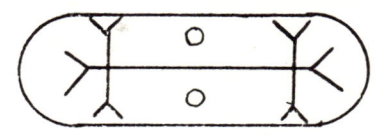

of which the true name is ZALŌZAKŌZ, and the interpretation ZKHŌZOZŌ. And when Jesus had finished; even at that moment the Arkhons took away their iniquities from the disciples; and these rejoiced with a great joy that the iniquity of the Arkhons had ceased in them. And when the iniquity of the Arkhons no longer existed in them, the disciples who followed Jesus became immortal in all the places that they entered.

Jesus said unto his disciples:

"I will give you the word of Power in all places of which I have given you the mystery, the baptisms, the offerings, the seals, the Paralēmptōr, and the number, the Names of Truth and the Words of Power, also the manner in which it is necessary to invoke them so that you may enter into their hidden places. I will give you the Words of Power and the numbers. Hear me now in order that I may speak unto you of the going forth of your soul, since I have revealed these mysteries, their seals, and their numbers. When thou goest forth from thy body and performest the mysteries of all the Æons and those which are in them, they shall fly before you until you come to the Six Great Æons. They shall fly to the west and to the left hand. When you have come to the Six Æons you will be stopped until you have received the mystery of the remission of sins, for this is the great mystery which is in the Æon of the Holy of Holies, and giveth health to the soul. He who has received this mystery shall surpass all gods and all lords and all Æons which are the Twelve Æons of the Invisible God, because this is the Great Mystery of the Immutable One who is in the Æon of the Holy of Holies. This is why all men who believe in the Son of Light must receive the mystery of the remission of sins. . . . And when all the Æons have fled before you the Light of the Purifying Æon will purify the twelfth Æon, so that all thy ways may be illuminated, and the Æon of Light may manifest, that you may behold the heavens from afar and the Paths of Light. . . . When you have received these mysteries, and you go hither and thither, having gone forth from the body you will become a pure Light, and you will journey even unto the Æon of Light."

Jesus then described unto his disciples the nature of the Æons of Light.

And His disciples said unto Jesus:

"Oh, Lord, why do all these habitations exist, or rather the Fatherhood which is in them? Why do they exist with the hierarchies which they contain? Why do they exist, and why do we exist?"

Jesus answered them and said:

"These things exist by reason of a Little Thought which is without the Father. He has not drawn it towards himself; he has drawn unto himself all things saving only this Little Thought which is still without, and is not part of Him: I shone forth in this Little Thought; I sprang forth like a jet of water; I turned myself towards it; I shone forth in it; it brought me forth; I am the first of those who came forth from it; I am its Image and its likeness, now that I am come forth. I am in its presence. Again the Little Thought shone forth, it cried with another cry which was the second: this cry was heard in all the worlds, and then the second Emanation came forth; in its turn the second emanation went forth itself and followed those of its own likeness; it existed in all the worlds which had gone forth following their own likenesses. The little Thought had brought forth all these worlds. Again it cried with a third cry, and moved the emanation towards the virtue of the Æons, and all the princes of the world came into existence and were in their respective worlds from the first even unto the last. My Father Himself gave movement unto these chiefs; one by one did he bring forth the twelve emanations and distributed them into the worlds from the first unto the last of all the Treasures. Oh, my Disciples, I have shown you the holy places of these Abodes, and the hierarchies thereof in order that you might follow me into all the habitations that I may enter into, in order that you may serve me in all the places that I go into in order that I may call you my Disciples. Now then when you enter these places say the Names which I have taught you, with the seal with which you must sign yourselves; speak the name of the Seal and hold the number in your hand; and the guardians, the hierarchies and the firmaments will show you the way by which you may enter into the place of their paternity, and you will enter into the Interior even until you come unto the world of the God of Truth that is to say the Perfection of Treasures which I have made known unto you."

Then the Disciples of Christ said unto him:

"Lord, when we said, Give us a name which shall suffice for all the worlds, you answered us and said, When I have passed through all the worlds and have brought you forth from them, then I will tell it unto you. Now behold we have traversed all the worlds and we have seen all that they contain; you have taught us their names and the names of their seals, and their numbers so that they shall open before us from the first even unto the last; teach us then that Name of which you have spoken in order that we may speak it in all the worlds of the Æons, and that they may open before us."

Then Jesus said unto them:

"Hear ye then and I will tell you, guard it in your heart."

Then they said:

"Is this the Great Name of your Father, who existed from the Beginning, or of one greater?"

And the Christ said:

"No, but it is the Name of the Great Force which is in all worlds. If you speak the word, all the Worlds must submit. Those which are in the Æons from the first to the last, even unto the Treasure of the God of Truth. The Guardians, the Hierarchies, and the Firmaments shall open before you; this is the name which I tell unto you:

AAAŌŌŌZŌRAZAZZZAIEŌZAZAEEEIIIZAIEŌZŌAKHŌEOOOYTHŌ-EZAOZAEZÈÈÈZZÈÈZAOZAKHŌZAÈKHEYEITYXAALETHYKH.

"This is the Name which you must speak in the interior world; the Name of the God of Truth is an exterior world. Live then in the exterior world, pronounce this name, mark yourself with the seal of which the Name is ZZEEŌŌKHAAAEZAZA. Say it and take in your hands the number ZŌNSTTH. When you have arrived at your destination, pronounce this name, say it first, then turn towards the four quarters of the Holy Place, make the sign of the Seal, say the name of which you hold the number in your hands."

This is as much as it seems necessary to quote of the Gnostic papyrus.

In conclusion I will point out that to man destiny is often represented by his own fatal instincts; instincts which mislead him on every possible occasion. Guided by them the drowning man throws up his hands; the angry man clenches his fists, tightens up his muscles and becomes inarticulate; the young gather the fruits of life before they are ripe; the old shut themselves away from the flow of life and die of stagnation. Perverted instinct is the curse of the human race.

Now the seat of instinct is the heart, according to all ancient systems, and in the 125th Chapter of the *Book of the Dead*, the vessel of the heart was weighed in the balance against a feather or image of truth, that is to say, against the power of perception.

To the Egyptians of old the cultivation of discernment was the aim of life, the want of it was a deadly sin in their eyes, and ended in the annihilation of the individuality. To gain perception of Truth, and so guide these fatal instincts, was the object of initiation. From the first step even, the Aspirant was taught to look upon himself as the centre of a universe of instinctive force, made on the pattern of the vast universe of which he formed a microscopic portion. Over him brooded the wings of the invisible—his pleroma filled with the attributes of his divinity, as the universe is filled with the rays of the light-givers. Daily the initiate studied the names, and meditated on the inward significance of the sounds and forms symbolizing the habitations of the Æons of the Absolute within this pleroma. And to carry the correspondences further, the capitals of the nomes of Egypt each represented a station in the Divine Hierarchy (compare the eighteenth chapter of the *Book of the Dead*). Gods also were assigned to the twenty-one parts of the human body (compare the forty-second chapter of the *Book of the Dead*). It is in the persistence of these ideas that we get one strong link between the ancient Egyptians and the Gnostics. They both also believed in the efficacy of fixed thought and the repeated word. The continual assertion of the virtues and powers of the King, for instance, was not mere flattery, but was believed to really induce virtues and powers in the monarch. By the same means the priests gained power by the identification of themselves with the types of natural forces, known to us as gods. The conviction that must accompany the assertions of innocence made in the Judgment Hall of Truth, answered very nearly to the later doctrine of the forgiveness of sins by faith. This may also be compared to the initiation into the mystery of the forgiveness of sins mentioned above in the quotations from the Bruce Papyrus.

The first necessity of the study of Magic among the Egyptians was the cultivation of all the faculties dormant in human nature. For they considered human power was only limited by weakness of will, and poverty of imagination. The Will-Energy, and Imaginative-thought, are often symbolised by fire and water, and the power of the spirit by air the Qabalistic Ruach. These are the divine Trinity of Father, Mother and Son (sometimes called Heaven, Earth and Mankind). The three Baptisms of the Bruce Papyrus bear a distinct analogy to the gifts of air, water and fire described in the *Book of the Dead*, chapters liv.-lxiii.

Finally the Magic of the Egyptians was founded on an elaborate scheme of the universe; and the interaction of natural forces was most carefully observed and studied. Of course it seems absurd to us to make a mystery of the real length of the year, or of the fact that the sun was the central body of the universe, or of the power of a man of vital force to hypnotise or mesmerise a feebler formulation of the chaos from which he himself and the whole universe is evolved. But for the priesthood of Egypt the knowledge of these facts included the conviction of the deep significance of their analogies, and of the powers such knowledge gave. At the same time we must remember that these men and women were Practical Rulers, bent on keeping the power that they held; and had they possessed the secret of dynamite they would certainly not have revealed it to the multitude.

Such was the Magic of Egypt during forty centuries of greatness, and now what remains? Let us look to Shelley for our answer. He tells us:

> I met a traveller from an antique land
> Who said: "Two vast and trunkless legs of stone
> Stand in the desert. Near them on the sand,
> Half sunk a shattered visage lies, whose frown
> And wrinkled lip and sneer of cold command,
> Tell that its sculptor well those passions read
> Which yet survive, stamped on these lifeless things,
> The hand that mocked them and the heart that fed.
> And on the pedestal these words appear.
> 'My name is Ozymandias, King of kings;
> Look on my works, ye mighty, and despair!'
> Nothing beside remains. Round the decay
> Of that colossal wreck, boundless and bare,
> The lone and level sands stretch far away.'

THE END.

STUDIES IN HERMETIC TRADITION

It is becoming more and more apparent that the esoteric tradition, far from being a cultural aberration, has expressed many of the deepest and abiding aspirations of Western civilization and that in many cases it may be seen as an illuminating complement to rather than an opponent of rational scientific thinking.

The aim of the STUDIES IN HERMETIC TRADITION series is to provide the student and the general reader with the texts of key, and often neglected, works in the field of occult philosophy and hermetic science in order to stimulate discussion and encourage the serious academic investigation of the Western esoteric tradition.

Titles so far published are:

THE BOOK OF SPLENDOURS
Eliphas Lévi
An examination of the inner mysteries of Qabalism and its relationship to Freemasonry, numerology and the Tarot.

THE CHALDEAN ORACLES OF ZOROASTER
Introduction by Kathleen Raine
A set of epigrammatic utterances or 'oracles' attributed to ancient Chaldean magicians and covering such subjects as the nature of God, demons, the soul, elemental forces and magical precepts.

THE DREAM OF SCIPIO (SOMNIUM SCIPIONIS)
Introduction by Robert Temple
Part of the 'Collectenea Hermetica' series, published under the editorship of W. Wynn Westcott from 1893-6. This volume contains an English translation of the *Somnium Scipionis* by Percy Bullock as well as other Greek Mystery texts.

THE GREAT SECRET
Eliphas Lévi
A treatise on magnetism, astral emanations, divination and creative omnipotence.

THE MYSTERIES OF THE QABALAH
Eliphas Lévi
An examination of the occult relationship between the Old Testament Prophecies of Ezekiel and the New Testament Revelation of St John.

THE QABALAH
Papus
A classic disquisition on the sacred science of the Hebrews and esoteric Christian teachings.